Man and Environment Series
Editor: David Burtenshaw

Cities and Towns

David Burtenshaw

UNWIN HYMAN

Published by
UNWIN HYMAN LIMITED
15/17 Broadwick Street
London W1V 1FP

First published in 1983 by Bell & Hyman Limited

Reprinted 1986, 1989

British Library Cataloguing in Publication Data

Burtenshaw, David
Cities and towns.—(Man and environment series)
1. Cities and towns.
I. Title II. Series
910′.091732 GF125

ISBN 0 7135 1366 7

Phototypeset by Tradespools Ltd, Frome, Somerset.
Printed and bound in Great Britain by
Butler & Tanner Ltd, Frome and London

Contents

Acknowledgements

The germ of this text was the product of discussions with Chris Kington of the publishers although the final content has been my responsibility. Ideas, assistance and inspiration have come from many sources and I hope that those who I have missed will feel recompensed on seeing their ideas in print. I am indebted in particular to Michael Bateman and Graham Moon at Portsmouth Polytechnic, for their assistance and criticism and to colleagues at Carleton University, Ottawa who made me aware of many of the Canadian studies and examples. Ann and Linda Garnett translated my scrawl and Paul Allingham had the unenviable task of compiling the maps from my drafts. Caroline Paines was a most patient shepherd of the work through the publishing process. My family, and especially Helen, have visited many of the locations with me, waiting while I found the shopping centre plan or the map. Finally I wish to dedicate the book to the citizens of the twenty-first century, not least my own children Christopher, Clare and Emma, for whom this book was conceived.

D.B. 1983

The author and the publishers wish to thank the following for permission to reproduce illustrations:
John Wiley & Sons Ltd from *The City in West Europe* by Burtenshaw and Bateman: Figures 2.13, 3.11, 3.12, 6.2, 6.4 and 6.5.
from *The Socialist City* by Hamilton: Figure 2.15
from *Interpreting the City* by Hartshorne: Figures 3.3, 5.10 and 5.12.
R Davies: Figure 3.5
P Daniels: Figure 3.6
A Hallsworth: Figure 4.3
S Pinch: Figures 7.11, 7.12 and 7.13

Acknowledgements are also due to the following sources from which illustrations have been adapted:
The Institute of British Geographers: Figures 1.11, 5.7, 5.8 and 7.7.
Oxford University Press: Figure 2.10
Harper & Row: Figures 3.14, 3.15 and 5.5
Macmillan, Canada and St Martin's Press: Figures 2.2c, 2.4 and 2.6
Her Majesty's Stationery Office: Figures 7.1, 7.2, 7.3 and 7.4 (all from *Unequal City*)
Pergamon Press Ltd: Figures 5.9 and 5.13
The Open University: Figure 7.10

Series preface

Alvin Toffler, in his book *Future Shock*, examined the effects of the increasing pace of change in modern society. The speed of change in modern geographical education to the 16–19 age group is no exception. The methodology of the Quantitative Revolution is commonplace and examination boards have now begun to encompass the more challenging framework of the People-Environment approach and the introduction of value-based learning. In addition, the nature of the traditional sixth form has been changed so that the traditional Advanced level student is not the sole type of student. Sixth form and tertiary colleges teaching large groups and the increasing numbers of students in the 'New Sixth' studying for BTEC, A/S and similar awards, are common today. In addition, only a small proportion of geographers at 16–19 actually proceed to take the subject in further education.

These contrasting demands have influenced the thinking behind this series of short texts aimed at the modern lower sixth student, ninety per cent of whom will not pursue geography beyond the sixth form. We have assumed that the readers will have taken GCSE geography examinations although the content should present no difficulties for the more mature reader. In all the texts it is our intention that the author's enthusiasm for the topic, combined with the interest generated by the presentation of the text, will assist a wide range of learners in and out of the classroom.

Every text can be studied in isolation, which should suit the individual curriculum of any group. Therefore, there is little attempt to cross reference texts which might be used in different order by schools and colleges. In addition, a self-standing set of texts leaves topic selection within a syllabus to the teacher's discretion. Nevertheless, the texts will develop new views of the more traditional sections of geography and introduce others where available material at this level is limited.

All the authors have a common concern for the improvement of geography teaching to the 16–19 group as experienced teachers, or lecturers, or examiners. All try to build on existing knowledge of our environment and to stress the dynamic nature of the environment. Where possible, they have asked the reader to express attitudes and explain values towards the major issues which affect our social, economic and physical environment. Above all, the authors are aware of geography's continuing role in teaching people how to think.

David Burtenshaw
Waterlooville 1983

Urban geography – what is it?

Today I left my detached house in suburbia and on the way to my work by car took my children to school. I reached work late because of a traffic jam where the urban motorway ends. I worked in my college, close to the centre of the city, all day and visited the city centre bank in my lunchtime. This evening I visited the superstore with my wife because it is open late. We also took one of our children to train at an athletics club.

All these activities of one family living in suburban Portsmouth are structured within the built environment of the city and take place at specific places in the city. It is the location of families like mine and the location of activities and functions within the town or city which are the major focus of urban geography. Merely describing land uses, journeys and locations however does not lead us very far. We need to understand why people live in a detached house, ten miles away from their work place. Is it because everyone in education is rich? Or is it because this is an area where we could buy our house with a study where I can write this book? Is it because I like the area or because the Building Society prefer to lend money to people who want to move to the areas which they like for investment purposes? Urban geography seeks to offer explanations not only for distributions of homes but for all the facilities which we associate with urban life.

We also need these days to be aware of the problems posed for our urban society. The reason why my morning journey is punctuated by a stop-start crawl listening to the local radio station is that opposition to new motorways in cities has grown. The residents of the inner city now bitterly oppose new roads which bulldoze away homes for the sake of the wealthy commuter. Road schemes are held up by such conflicts and the urban geographer of today must be aware of this kind of issue. Similarly, we need to be aware of other changes such as the new types of shop with their evening opening hours, the benefits which they might bring to the mobile and the problems which the disabled have of reaching them. Urban geography is, therefore, not just about the buildings of a town or city and their functions; *it is the study of the patterns of economic and social activity in both time and space*. Time is important for the city is used differently at weekends or at night.

It is the intention of this text to try to explore and explain some of the patterns and activities of towns and cities. Because our understanding of places begins from our home town I have tried to work from known examples in Great Britain to examples which one might easily see on holiday in Europe and North America and out to the world further afield.

From now on when terms and concepts are first introduced they will be in bold or heavy type, coupled with a definition. I have also posed questions and suggestions for discussion which you may like to pursue besides exercises which could form the basis of a later project. I wondered whether to give answers but I hope that you will be able to distinguish those questions where the answer is apparent in the text and those where opinions vary and debate of the issue aids understanding. Only by debating the questions which have been posed in this text can we begin to understand the complex issues of our urban society and be in a position to be informed about the cities in which we live.

1
Urbanisation

The great majority of people in Britain today live in towns and cities, or if they do not live in the city, they work there or depend on the nearby town or city for shopping and other facilities. We tend to take the fact that there is a town near us for granted. However, the process of becoming an urban society – **urbanisation** – was very significant in Britain and Western Europe during the nineteenth century, and in North America during the last decades of the nineteenth century and the early twentieth century. Urbanisation is a phenomenon today in the developing countries of the **third world** and many parts of what we will term the **socialist world** (the USSR and Eastern Europe) and the **communist world** (China). The questions that urban geographers have asked are as follows:

1 What phenomena do we associate with urbanisation?
2 Is urbanisation today the same as it was over a hundred years ago?
3 Is urbanisation in present day Africa or Asia the same as it was in Western Europe and North America?

Urbanisation in nineteenth century Britain

Since the early eighteenth century the rural societies of Western Europe have been profoundly changed from dependence on an agricultural economy to dependence on the production of a wide variety of industrially produced commodities from factories located mainly in towns. This process of **urbanisation** was associated with the Industrial Revolution. The coincidence of a growing population, growing markets at home and abroad, increasing wealth and the ability to harness the revolutionary technological developments of the age, such as steam and electric power, produced the economic conditions which attracted large numbers of people to live near the factories producing the new specialised commodities. In England and Wales this was a long process.

Cardiff is a good example of a city which exploded in population and area during the major period of urbanisation in nineteenth century Britain. Between 1801 and 1901 it changed from being a **pre-industrial city** of only 1870 people, living within the confines of the medieval walled town, to an **industrial city** of 164 333 persons (Figure 1.1). It was the growth of South Wales as the leading region of iron production and the leading area of steam coal

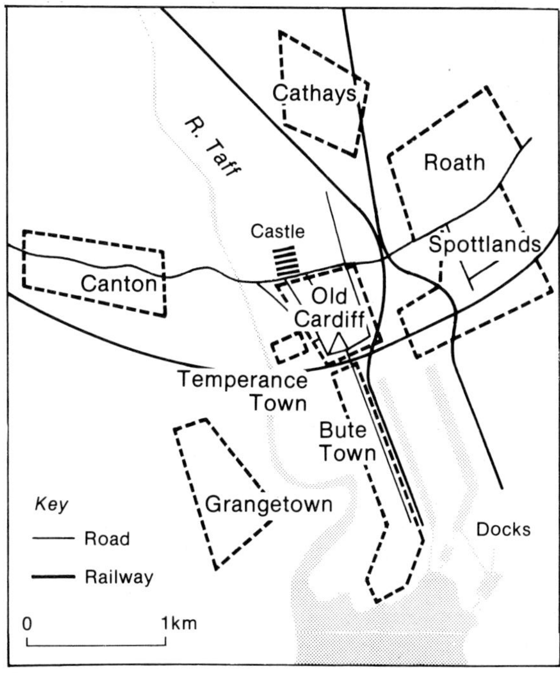

Figure 1.1 Nineteenth century Cardiff

production in Britain which resulted in Cardiff developing into a major coal-exporting port. The digging of a canal, the building of docks by the Bute family and the coming of the railways between 1836 and 1853 all aided the growth of the port. As construction and trade grew so more people were needed to work in the docks and the city.

The new working population came from near and far. The 1851 census showed that 13% of households in the city at that time came from the city. A third of the households came from the nearest counties of Glamorgan and Monmouth. The other major areas that supplied the migrants to the city were in South Wales or around the Bristol Channel. Table 1.1 shows how the urbanising process attracted immigrants from Ireland, who were fleeing famine, to come and live in Cardiff, initially as lodgers in seriously overcrowded conditions. They originated mainly from Cork and Waterford and came to gain employment.

Table 1.1 Origins of the population of Cardiff in 1851

	Heads and Wives %	Lodgers %	Servants %
Cardiff	12.58	7.95	16.26
Glamorgan	24.73	11.00	24.93
Monmouth	7.57	3.64	7.05
Carmarthen and Pembroke	8.23	6.43	8.67
Gloucester and Somerset	14.68	10.16	15.45
Ireland	11.57	38.24	9.49

The impact of the rise of industry and trade on the city was dramatic. New areas such as Newtown grew and were described in 1855 as follows:

'It has a low level; the streets have recently been pitched (surfaced); the houses for the most part are occupied as Irish lodging-houses, and are seriously overcrowded.'

By 1876 this area besides Splottlands had developed into suburbs for the working population. The better areas were normally along the main routes radiating from the town while the poorer properties lay behind. Bute Town still had high concentrations of lodgers and Canton to the west generally had better housing. Other suburbs such as Cathays and Roath were growing fast while Grangetown contained very poor housing.

Study activity

Select and draw diagrams or maps to illustrate the main sources of Cardiff's population in 1851. Which diagram or map best illustrates the origins of the urban population?

This quick picture of urbanisation in nineteenth century Cardiff points to several characteristics of the process:

1 Urbanisation took place partly as a result of the rapid increase of population following the better control of disease. It was therefore a demographic phenomenon which is the most common interpretation of the term.

2 More importantly, migration was a major factor both (i) from the surrounding areas with the proportion of migrants declining rapidly with distance from Cardiff (this is known as a **distance decay function** ie the decline of a pattern of migrants with distance; sometimes called a **distance lapse rate**) and (ii) as a result of immigration from Ireland pushed by rural poverty and famine.

3 The *pull* factors in Cardiff were the new trading and commercial role of the city and the jobs available both in these activities and in the construction industry, especially digging the docks.

4 The city exploded outwards to a series of suburbs of differing quality with the signs of distinct areas developing. This growth was aided by improved transport.

Although Cardiff did not grow as rapidly during the period of urbanisation as other

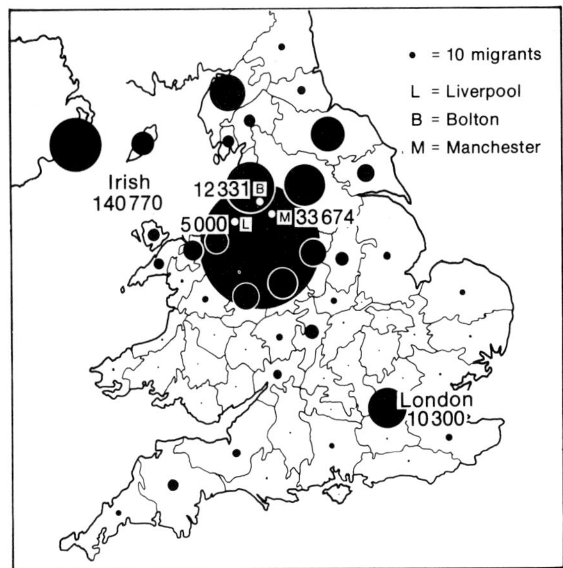

Figure 1.2 Migration into Bolton, Manchester and Liverpool, 1851 (after Redford)

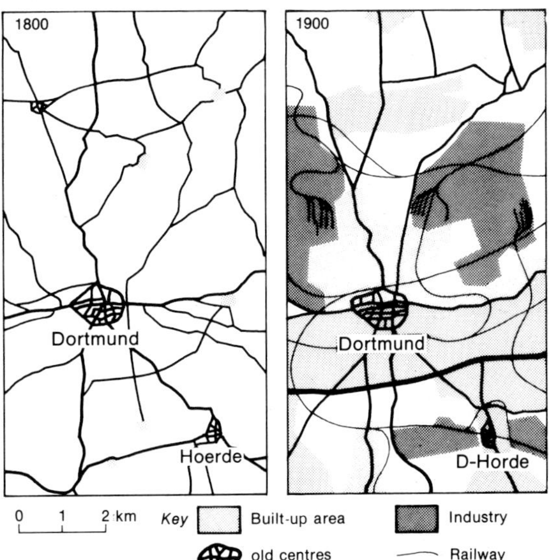

Figure 1.3 Dortmund, 1800 and 1900

towns and cities in Britain, similar processes operated at different times during the industrial revolution and with differing intensity. Migration into Liverpool, Manchester and Bolton is shown on Figure 1.2. This was much larger in scale than Cardiff as the specialised industries of the Lancashire towns and cities sucked labour in and housed them in high density terrace rows and backcourts. Oldham grew from 21000 in 1801 to 137000 in 1901 and Manchester from 75000 to 544000 in the same period. It was not long before the towns of south-east Lancashire expanded to such an extent that they began to merge with each other, so much so that by 1915 Sir Patrick Geddes, the prioneer urban scientist, had coined the term **conurbation** for the growing together of settlements. West Yorkshire, Tyneside, Glasgow, Birmingham and the Black Country were other rapidly urbanising conurbations at that time.

Engels in his text *The Condition of the Working Class in England*, published in 1845, described the consequences of urbanisation in the major cities most graphically.

'These slums are pretty equally arranged in all the great towns of England, the worst houses in the worst quarters of the towns; usually one or two storied cottages in long rows, perhaps with cellars used as dwellings, almost always irregularly built.'

Urbanisation in the nineteenth century had produced over 150 cities of over 100000 population in Europe and North America compared with only 22 in Europe alone a century earlier. A large industrial conurbation was growing rapidly in the German Ruhr area where the new mining, iron and steel and metallurgical industries brought about the expansion of Dortmund (Figure 1.3), Essen and Bochum beside new workers settlements associated with mines and works such as Bottrop, Gladbeck and Wanne-Eickel. Urbanisation was also a social process because it changed the pattern of social life from one centred on a rural society, dependent on family and kin, to a more stratified society of owners and workers. A new way of life dependent on the selling of labour, the payment of a wage and the independent existence of the wage-earner and family developed. It was argued that social life was less close-knit and more dependent on casual friendship. Therefore, the process of urbanisation produced the separation of work and residence and of residential groups which mirrored in its areal form the new industrial society of owners and workers.

Urbanisation in North America

The role of industrial growth in the process of urbanisation was stressed by Pred in his study of the growth of American cities in the period 1860 to 1910. Pred has shown how the introduction of a factory industry into a small trading community earned the community money. These new earnings for the town had a **multiplier effect** in that they were used to pay for new services, such as banks, so employing more people. Industries which were linked to the new factory would be attracted so that, for instance, abbatoirs and meat packing attracted tanneries to process the hides into leather. These activities created further demand in the town which encouraged the factory owners to expand production and to develop more new industry. At the same time growth in output encouraged the development of new, more efficient production techniques which would raise profits. Thus invention or innovation in its turn helped industry to expand. Pred called this a process of **cumulative causation**, and he suggested that this continued unabated until competition from another city or the city's size and its economic activities were too unwieldy and suffered from **diseconomies** ie. the costs of production rise because of higher costs resulting from congestion and other factors. The process would also stop and perhaps reverse if the basis of initial growth vanished as happened with many mining settlements.

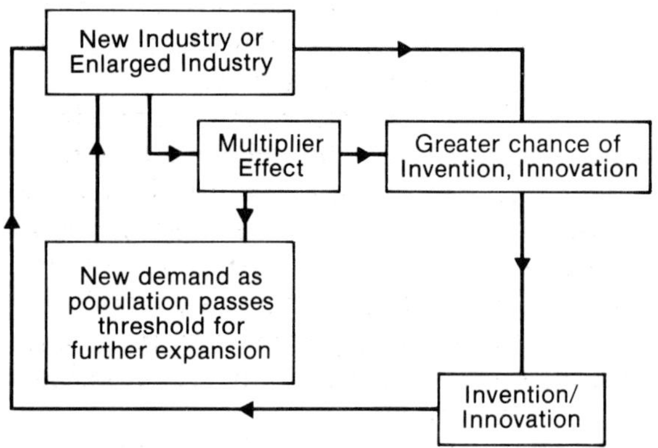

Figure 1.4 *Pred's model of cumulative causation*

Study activity

Study maps of your town or city during the nineteenth century which are often found in the Record Office or main library's reference section. When did the major spatial growth take place? Was the spatial growth paralled by increases in the town's population? (Local histories or the censuses would probably contain the figures.) What industrial or commercial developments caused the growth?

Urbanisation in the third world

Urbanisation today is still continuing very rapidly but not in Europe, North America and the developed western world. Figure 1.5 shows that the proportion of population living in urban areas, as defined by the United Nations, is growing more rapidly than in any previous period. If we look closely at the pattern of urbanisation since 1950 it is the urban population of Africa, Latin America and Asia which has grown most rapidly in numbers. (Figure 1.6 and Table 1.2). In Africa the urban population grew by 5.5% per annum between 1950 and 1975 and still

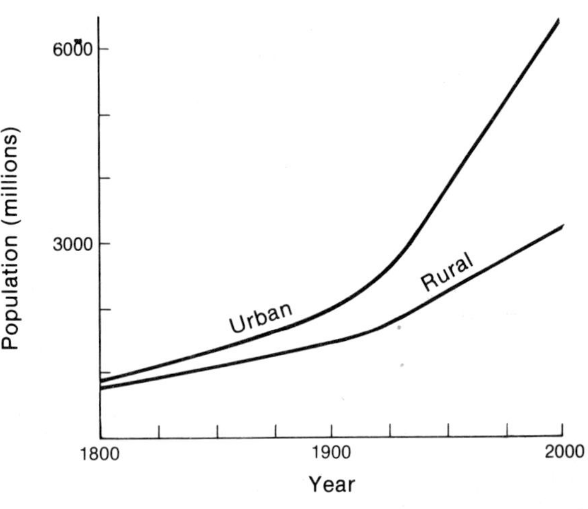

Figure 1.5 *The growing proportion of population living in urban areas (UN)*

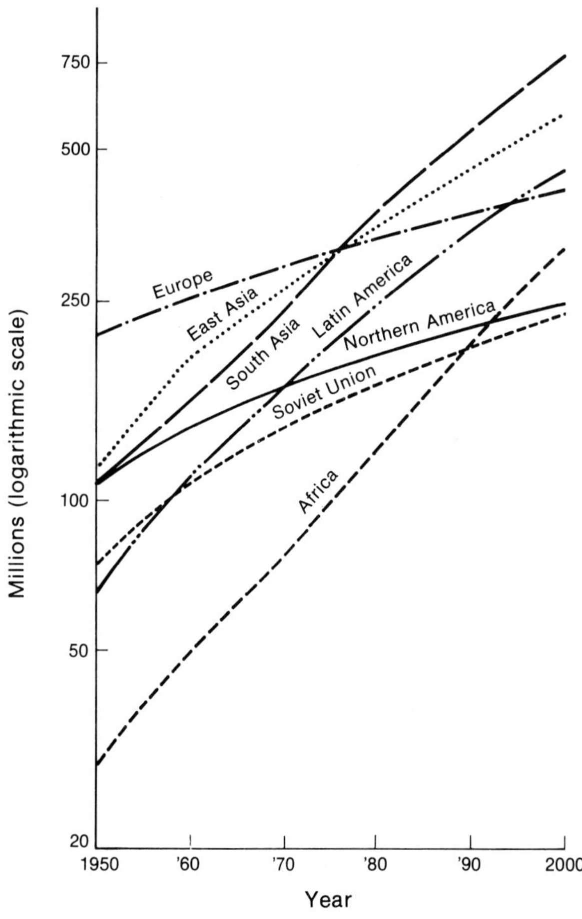

Figure 1.6 *Urban population growth by continental regions*

Table 1.2 Percentage of urban dwellers in total population

	1950	1975
North America	63.6	76.5
Oceania	64.5	71.6
Europe	54.8	67.2
Soviet Union	39.4	60.5
Latin America	40.9	60.4
East Asia	16.6	30.7
Africa	13.2	24.4
South Asia	15.5	23.0

only a quarter of the population live in towns. The population explosion combined with the explosive growth of the cities for a selection of African countries is shown in Table 1.3. These figures do no more than

Table 1.3 Urbanisation levels in selected African countries

	Population 1950 000	Total Urban %	Population 1975 000	Total Urban %	Average Annual Urban Growth Rate %
Africa	204672	11	373439	23	5.5
Egypt	20461	32	37543	48	4.0
Nigeria	34331	10	62925	18	4.7
Ghana	5024	14	9873	32	5.8
Ivory Coast	2822	6	4885	20	6.8
Zaire	13055	8	24485	26	7.1
Zambia	2473	11	5022	37	7.5
Zimbabwe	2276	10	6276	20	6.5

make us aware of the speed and scale of third world urbanisation, a fact which was recognised by the United Nations Vancouver Declaration on Human Settlements. The Declaration of Principles states

'the circumstances of life for vast numbers of people in human settlements are unacceptable, particularly in developing countries. Unless positive and concrete action is taken at national and international levels to find and implement solutions these conditions may be further aggravated as a result of . . . uncontrolled urbanisation and consequent conditions of overcrowding, pollution, deterioration and psychological tensions in metropolitan regions'.

It would seem that little had changed since Engels described the consequences of urbanisation in London. However we need to ask whether the process is identical to Britain and America over a century ago.

At first glance, urban growth in Africa or Asia to-day might resemble that of 1851 Britain. There is a flight from rural areas by people attracted to the cities, and the conditions which were outlined above seem similar. Urbanisation in the third world differs in one essential aspect; it is on the whole urbanisation without industrialisation. Mountjoy describes it as

'underemployment in the village is being exchanged for unemployment in the towns'.

The attempts to develop industry are relatively concentrated because the necessary **infrastructure** (transport and facilities such as waste disposal) is not there. Industry is associated most with the exploitation and processing of primary products such as minerals. Thus the towns of the Zambian copperbelt have grown in association with the exploitation of a resource. Enugu in Nigeria has also grown from no people in 1914 to 187000 on the basis of mining. Normally the facilities and infrastructure for industry are only available with any certainty in the capital city and the major port of the country, which may be the same place as is the case at Lagos (Figure 1.7). This former European trading post is now the national and federal state capital with a remarkable concentration of external investment, commerce and industry that attracts population from all over Nigeria.

In many third world countries the effect of the concentration of limited economic potential and thousands of immigrants into the capital city is to increase the capital's **primacy**. Primacy is the degree to which the first city dominates all others. Thus Dakar contains 16% of Senegal's population, 80% of its industrial workers and 70% of its commercial workers. If Zipf's **rank size rule** (which we will return to later) is correct then the population of the second city will be one half of that of the largest city. In fact, Dakar has a population of 798792 and the next largest town is Thiès with a mere 117333. Dakar has become a **primate city** because its size is twice what we might expect given the assumptions of the rank size rule.

One consequence of accelerating urbanisation is the **shanty town** or **spontaneous settlement** built of any available materials, lacking proper sanitation and any infrastructure (Figure 1.8). We shall return to this topic in greater detail in Chapter 5.

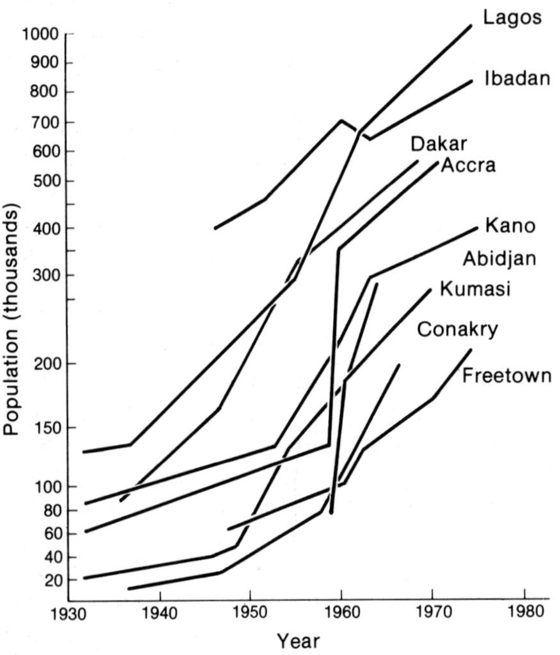

Figure 1.7 Population growth in West African towns (after Safier)

Study activity

1 You are the mayor of a small town (the fourth in size) of 40000 people in a tropical country dominated by a primate port city four times the size of two mining towns. You are 350 km from the capital and 200 km from the mining towns. How could you persuade the government to encourage migration to your town?

2 How would you slow down migration to cities in the Third World and what would be the consequences?

Urbanisation in the socialist world

Urbanisation in the Socialist World has followed a different set of paths. In the more industrialised countries, such as the German Democratic Republic (East Germany), Poland and parts of Czechoslovakia, there were already large urban/industrial cities by 1945. In the case of the USSR only 15% of the population were urbanised in 1945 but by the 1970s 56% were urbanised. Much of the

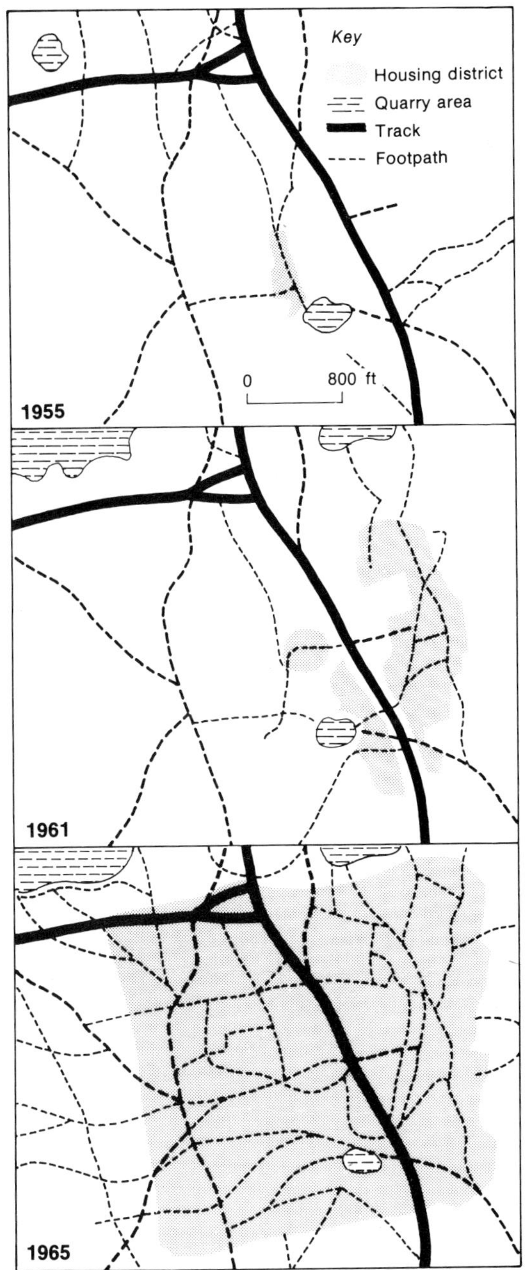

Figure 1.8 *Growth of a shanty near Lusaka*

urbanisation in the USSR has been associated with the rush to modernise and create a Soviet Marxist industrial economy. It has been an eastward push of urbanisation in the last fifty years which has mirrored the westward spread a century earlier in North America. The main urban foundations have been associated with major mineral discoveries especially coal, iron ore and oil. Cities such as Magnitogorsk mushroomed before World War II and after 1945 it was the Asian frontier cities which grew faster than the cities of southern California as Russians flocked to develop the new found mineral wealth.

The economic and social development of the area stretching east of the Urals from Sverdlovsk to Irkutsk was the responsibility of the central planning agencies aided by the Institute of Economics and Organisation of Industrial Production in Novosibirsk. Urbanisation was focused on a series of Territorial Production Complexes (Figure 1.9) or areas where mining, power production and associated basic industries were to be developed. Irkutsk is the focus of one such complex where hydroelectric power, coal mining, an aluminium smelter and later factories producing petro-chemicals, non-ferrous metals, building materials and food result in a current population which exceeds half a million.

Urban development further east in Siberia is dependent on the development of a new rail link, the Baykal-Amur Magistral (BAM) which will open up further resources. It is anticipated that the population of the western part of this area which was about 300000 in the mid-1970s will rise to over a million before the year 2000 as six or seven new territorial production complexes are developed.

Soviet urbanisation is very much the product of state planning. Lenin asked that rural and urban distinctions were removed and so efforts are made to blur the differences in opportunities and wages between the two. Great emphasis has been placed on efforts to control the size of the largest cities for instance by restricting migration to Moscow which already numbers seven million people and attracts half a million commuters from over 10 kilometres outside the city. **Greenbelts and forest belts** to limit physical growth are also favoured. The new urban areas have been constructed with the

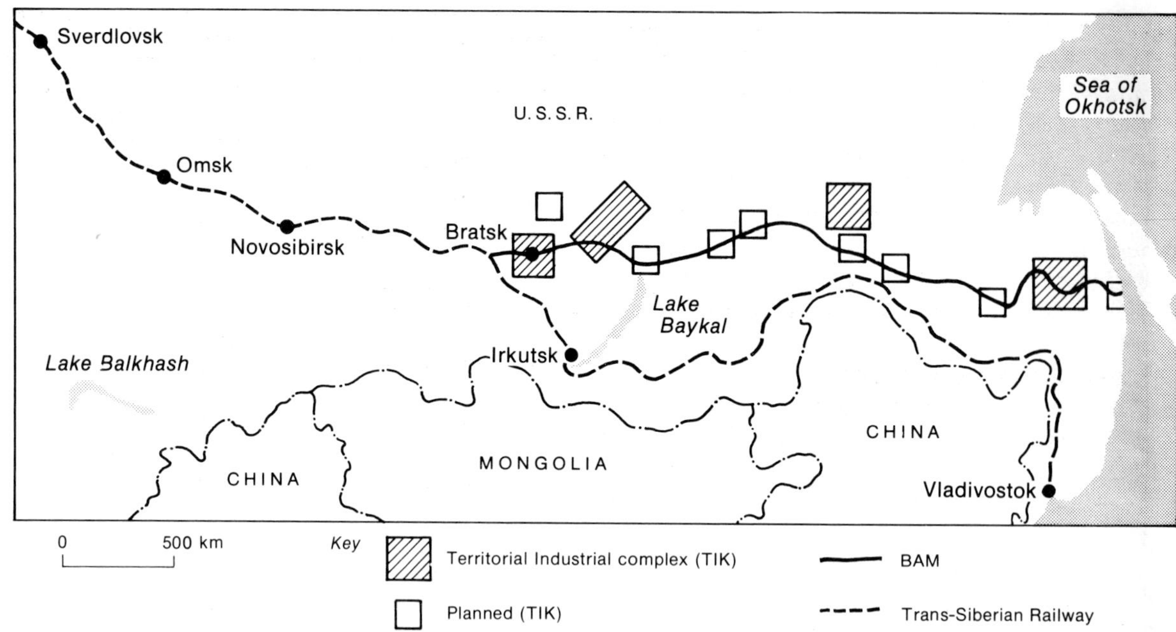

Figure 1.9 Territorial Production Complexes in Siberia since 1950

aim of developing a classless city so that the residential areas are low-cost, mass-produced three and four storey apartments with shops, schools, industry and recreation integrated into the schemes.

As we have noted many of the best examples of socialist urbanisation have taken place in **new towns**. It has been easier for the centralised state and party machines to create new towns which embody the ideals of communist thinking than to alter the pre-revolutionary cities. This is particularly the case in the more urbanised areas of Eastern Europe.

Urbanisation in the communist world

In the case of China urbanisation has followed a different path from that in the USSR mainly because of a dispute that has existed for over 50 years among socialist thinkers. Engels said:

'Civilisation has undoubtedly with its cities left us a heritage which will take much time and effort to eliminate; but it must and will be eliminated'.

This has been the path which Chinese communism under Mao Tse Tung followed although the Chinese, like the Russians, have favoured controlled urban-based development during several periods. The Marxist view dominated from 1966 until Mao's death so that planning was not centralised but came up from the bottom to the top and created much rural-based industrialisation without large bureaucracies to administer the system. By controlling the growth of administrators it was possible to control and even halt the growth of towns and cities. Today the urban population, while enormous by our standards at 140–150 million people, only represents 18% of the total population of the country and it has only expanded slightly from 15.4% in 1957. The four big cities, Guangzhou, Shanghai-Hangzhou, Tianjin-Beijing and Anshan-Fushun, have grown but many people in the cities still work in agriculture. They contain between 30 and 40% of industrial capacity. Large cities are restricted in growth to encourage growth in smaller centres and near major centres. At the same time the suburbs are to be made into **producing organisms**, that is, made more self-sufficient by encouraging market gardening in the new low density suburbs. The Chinese case, which has been sketched here, is that urbanisation is anti-communist. Marxist theory is anti-urban and the Chinese almost more than all others have pursued this utopian socialist ideal. There are those who have attempted to imitate this anti-urban position. The Khmer-Rouge on attaining power in Kampuchea in 1975 proceeded to evacuate the cities in order to radically change the way of life of Phnom Penh, the capitalist western style city, with most tragic consequences.

Urbanisation and counterurbanisation

With the possible exception of China we have seen that urbanisation in its many forms is a world-wide phenomenon. The process of becoming urban has resulted in the very rapid growth in the number of **millionaire cities**, ie. cities with over one million inhabitants, from 20 in 1900 to 213 in 1979 and the dominant locations of these have been drifting more towards the tropics. Urbanisation has produced in many areas either conurbations centred on the outward growth of one city or based on the expansion of several contiguous cities. The major metropolitan areas are listed in Table 1.4. Today, especially in the developed world, two further interrelated trends are also worth considering.

The first of these trends, because it was recognised earlier, is **megalopolitan urbanisation**. The existence of a **megalopolis** which can be defined as the merging of several conurbations and towns into a vast urbanised area which includes large areas of agricultural land and recreational areas was first coined by Gottman in 1961 in the United States. He noted how the eastern seaboard from Washington through Baltimore, Philadelphia and New York to Boston had grown into a vast urbanised area. Boswash, as it is called in the jargon, is one of three such areas in the United States (Figure 1.10); the others are Chipits (Chicago to Pittsburg including Detroit) and San San (San Francisco, Los Angeles and San Diego). Bourne attempted to define a fourth North American megalopolis stretching from Windsor, Ontario to Quebec City in Canada which he named Main Street. This area included Toronto, Ottawa and Montréal but it did not have the density of development or the patterns of economy and society that would make it a megalopolis.

Table 1.4 The major world cities in 1979

Rank	City area	Estimated population in millions
1	Tokyo-Yokohama	25.3
2	New York	16.8
3	Osaka-Kobe-Kyoto	15.0
4	Mexico City	13.7
5	São Paolo	11.3
6	Moscow	11.1
7	London	11.0
8	Calcutta	10.4
9	Buenos Aires	10.1
10	Seoul	9.9
11	Paris	9.4
12	Los Angeles	9.3
13	Rio de Janiero	9.1
14	Bombay	8.9
15	Cairo	8.5
16	Shanghai	8.3
17	Chicago	7.7
18	Manila	6.4
19	Jakarta	6.3
20	Delhi-New Delhi	5.8
21	Beijing	5.4
22	Tehran	5.3
23	Leningrad	5.3
24	Philadelphia	5.2
25	The Ruhr (Duisburg, Essen, Bochum, Dortmund)	5.1

Some people also try to see potential megalopolises in West Europe. In terms of the density of settlement much of the area bounded by Liverpool, Paris, Frankfurt and Amsterdam is more developed than the North American examples but there are major intervening areas which are still primarily rural such as northern France and central West Germany. Nevertheless both the Dutch and West German planners do refer to the possible expansion of the Dutch-Randstad conurbation and the Rhine-Ruhr conurbation to form a megalopolis Lower Rhine.

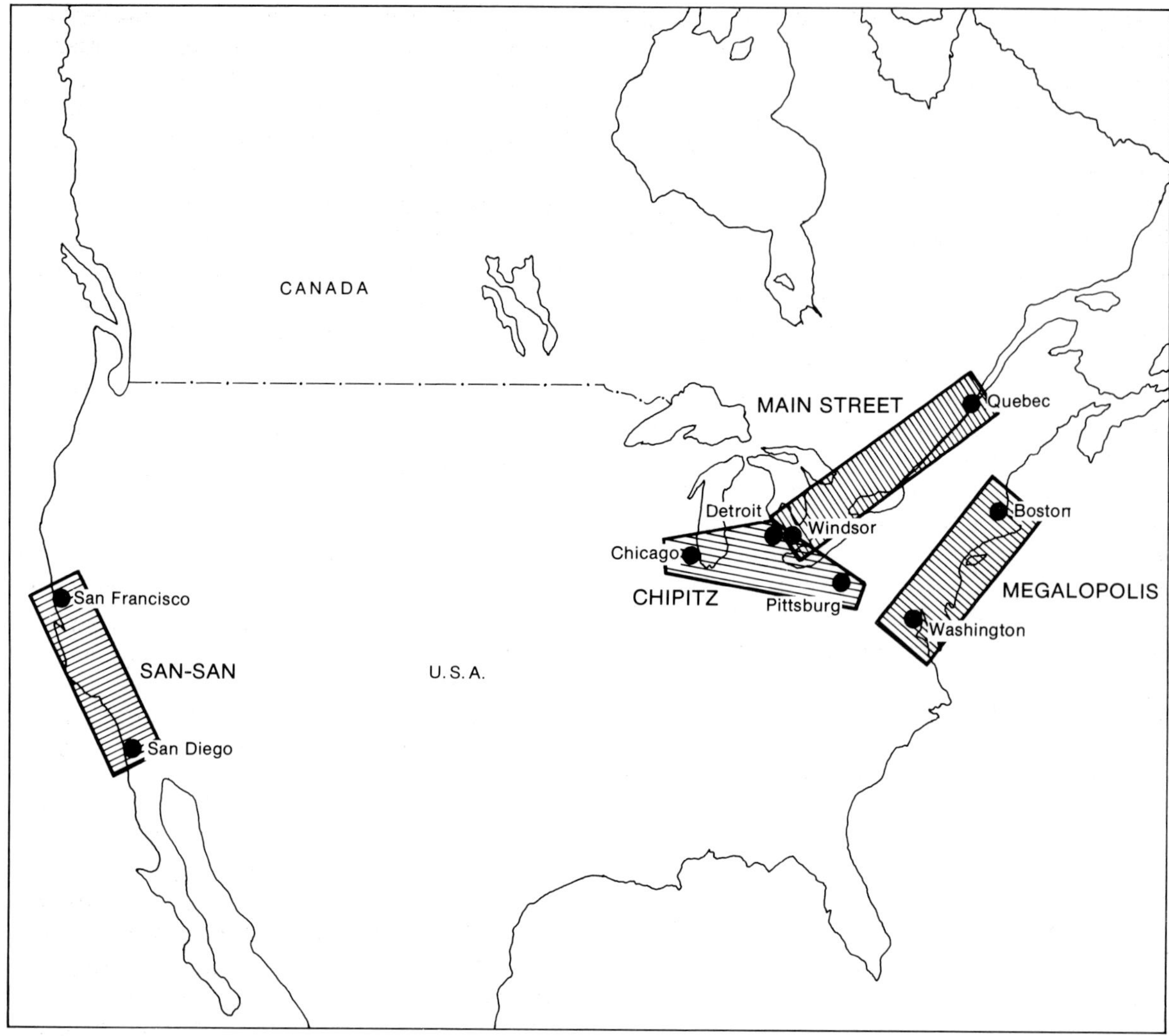

Figure 1.10 Megalopolitan areas in North America

The second trend is very much related to the first. The concept of **counterurbanisation** was developed by Berry in the United States and since applied in Western Europe. In studying the growth and change of North American cities Berry noted that much of the growth of a megalopolis was caused by the outward migration of the working population of cities so that people were travelling greater distances to work. (We will return to this topic in Chapter 4). The areas which provided the labour for cities were termed Standard Metropolitan Labour Areas (SMLAs) and these were spreading rapidly between 1950 and 1970 so that people of a city were living at increasingly low densities in semi-urban environments. This lowering of densities in the city and the slight raising of densities up to 50 miles from cities such as Chicago or New York is what Berry terms counterurbanisation.

Similar trends have been noted in Western Europe especially in Great Britain, Scandinavia, West Germany and the Netherlands. For instance Manchester lost 23% of its population between 1951 and 1971 and

Liverpool 24% in the same period as people migrated to live beyond the city's administrative boundary. The Europeans prefer to see counterurbanisation as a fourth phase in an urban development process (i) Urbanisation (ii) Urbanisation-Suburbanisation (iii) Suburbanisation (the current phase in much of Europe which we will examine in Chapter 4) and (iv) **desuburbanisation** when the agglomerations lose population and the regions gain population. The process of decentralisation are slower in Mediterranean Europe and France. Nevertheless, there are parallels between southern Europe and the south and west of the USA.

There is a modern growth of what can be termed **sun belt cities**. Low density cities in the States such as Dallas, Houston and Los Angeles have their counterparts in smaller but equally rapidly-expanding towns and cities such as Montpellier, Lyons, Barcelona, Genoa in sun belt Europe, although the population here is still centralising. Hall suggests that there is a series of stages in the process of urbanisation/counterurbanisation led by North America and then followed by Britain. As yet the evidence is still sketchy and Hall is unable to obtain clear trends in Europe. Bearing in mind that we noted intercontinental variations in urbanisation through time, it may be premature to expect the counterurbanisation or desuburbanisation process to follow the same course in Western Europe as in the United States. The higher overall densities of population and the environmental lobby supporting the preservation of an agricultural landscape and compact cities might result in a different process.

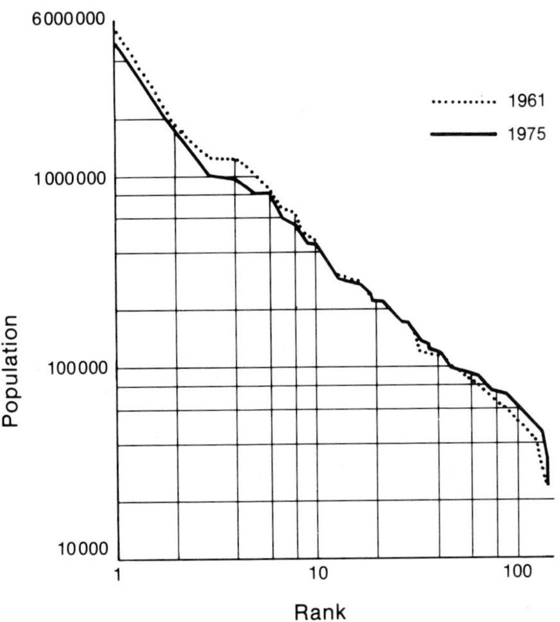

Figure 1.11 Rank size of cities in Great Britain, 1961 and 1975

Study questions

1 Distinguish between urbanisation and counterurbanisation.
2 Using an atlas attempt to delimit a megalopolis in Great Britain. Try to justify your area or lack of one. What, if any, is its outline?
3 What similarities are there between the Chinese attitude to urbanisation and counterurbanisation?

The national urban system

The product of the whole process of urbanisation is a **national urban system** which is the network of cities of varying size, ranking and relative spacing which changes through time. Here we can briefly examine two methods of looking at the urban system.

The most frequently used overview of a national urban system used by geographers is that of the **rank size rule** which we noted on page 12. Here the size and ranking of cities is plotted to see whether in reality the size of cities in a country is arrayed in a neat pecking order where the second city is half the size of the first and the nineteenth 1/19 the size. When plotted on logarithmic graph paper the theoretical distribution is a straight line and most countries vary from this in some way. The rank-size distribution for Britain has been plotted on Figure 1.11 and in Table 1.5. You can see how cities changed their rankings between 1961 and 1971.

Table 1.5 **The ranking of British cities**

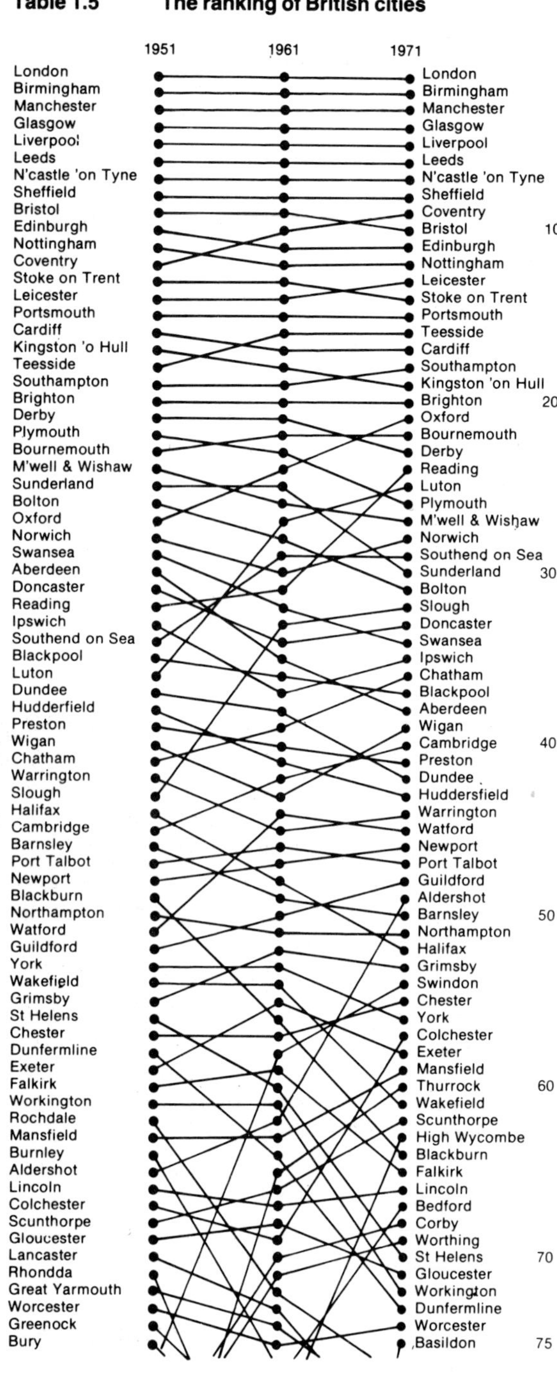

1951	1971	
London	London	
Birmingham	Birmingham	
Manchester	Manchester	
Glasgow	Glasgow	
Liverpool	Liverpool	
Leeds	Leeds	
N'castle 'on Tyne	N'castle 'on Tyne	
Sheffield	Sheffield	
Bristol	Coventry	
Edinburgh	Bristol	10
Nottingham	Edinburgh	
Coventry	Nottingham	
Stoke on Trent	Leicester	
Leicester	Stoke on Trent	
Portsmouth	Portsmouth	
Cardiff	Teesside	
Kingston 'o Hull	Cardiff	
Teesside	Southampton	
Southampton	Kingston 'on Hull	
Brighton	Brighton	20
Derby	Oxford	
Plymouth	Bournemouth	
Bournemouth	Derby	
M'well & Wishaw	Reading	
Sunderland	Luton	
Bolton	Plymouth	
Oxford	M'well & Wishaw	
Norwich	Norwich	
Swansea	Southend on Sea	
Aberdeen	Sunderland	30
Doncaster	Bolton	
Reading	Slough	
Ipswich	Doncaster	
Southend on Sea	Swansea	
Blackpool	Ipswich	
Luton	Chatham	
Dundee	Blackpool	
Hudderfield	Aberdeen	
Preston	Wigan	
Wigan	Cambridge	40
Chatham	Preston	
Warrington	Dundee	
Slough	Huddersfield	
Halifax	Warrington	
Cambridge	Watford	
Barnsley	Newport	
Port Talbot	Port Talbot	
Newport	Guildford	
Blackburn	Aldershot	
Northampton	Barnsley	50
Watford	Northampton	
Guildford	Halifax	
York	Grimsby	
Wakefield	Swindon	
Grimsby	Chester	
St Helens	York	
Chester	Colchester	
Dunfermline	Exeter	
Exeter	Mansfield	
Falkirk	Thurrock	60
Workington	Wakefield	
Rochdale	Scunthorpe	
Mansfield	High Wycombe	
Burnley	Blackburn	
Aldershot	Falkirk	
Lincoln	Lincoln	
Colchester	Bedford	
Scunthorpe	Corby	
Gloucester	Worthing	
Lancaster	St Helens	70
Rhondda	Gloucester	
Great Yarmouth	Workington	
Worcester	Dunfermline	
Greenock	Worcester	
Bury	Basildon	75

1981 data has not been added because city boundaries changed in 1974
Numbers = place in 1951 or 1971

Study activity

1 Can you explain why cities moved up or down the rank-size hierarchy?
2 Rank the teams of the English football league at the end of a season from 92 at the top of Division I to 1 at the bottom of Division IV. Aggregate those teams in a city. To what extent does this give you a ranking of cities?
3 Can you explain the rise and fall in the rankings? Why were there so few changes at the top of the ranking?

As we saw when looking at third world urbanisation processes a **primate** pattern is found very frequently in the third world. On the other hand the destruction of a national hierarchy by the radical alteration of the national frontiers can create a primate situation as in the case of Austria after the First World War (Figure 1.12). Small countries are also more likely to develop a high degree of primacy as in Jersey, Luxembourg or even Denmark.

On the other hand other national systems are more complex and lack any ranking with two or more major centres dominating. This type of system characterises West Germany where the division of the country combined with the effects of a federal state has produced a very stepped hierarchy (Figure 1.12). The federal governmental system and the importance given to many towns may also account for the nature of the Swiss hierarchy.

If we return to the British hierarchy (Figure 1.11 and Table 1.5) you might have noted that, although there is a semblance of a ranking dominated by London, there is also a tendency for the rank-size line to be a series of steps. This does suggest that rather than a ranking of cities some form of crude hierarchy might be a better way of describing the urban system of Britain with more than one centre at each successive layer in the hierarchy. However, except in a few areas, the hierarchy of towns and cities is not regularly

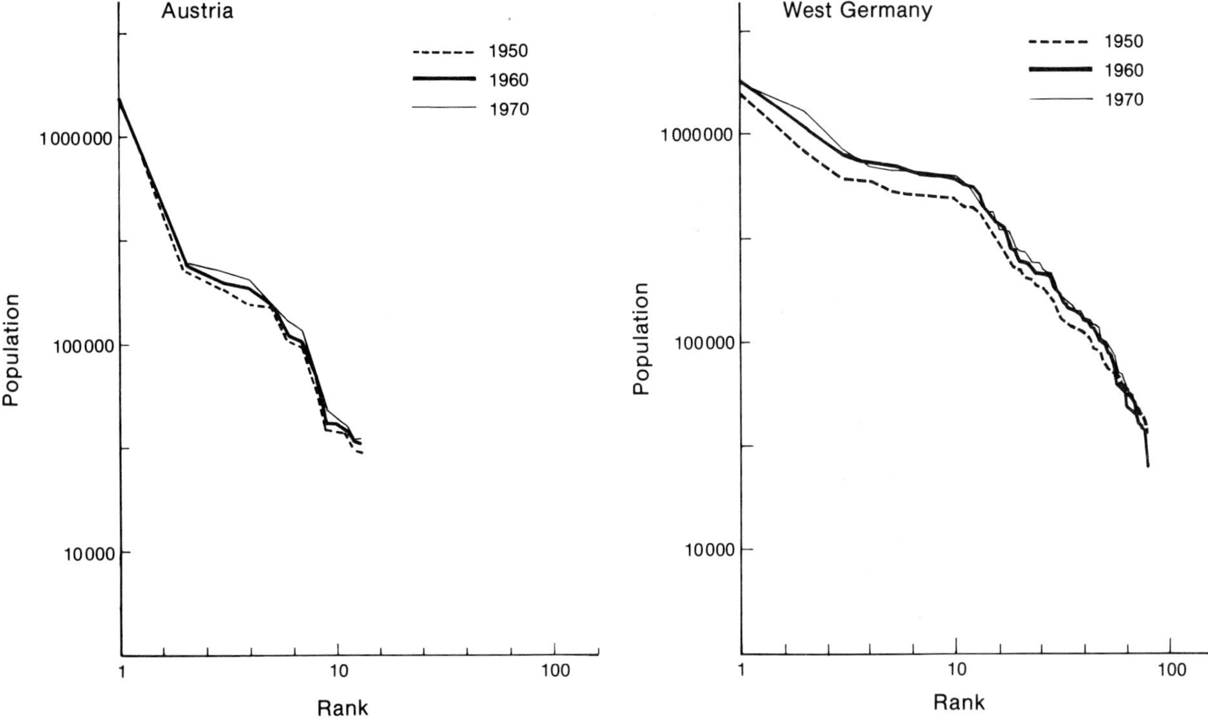

Figure 1.12 Rank size of cities in Austria and West Germany

spaced as Christaller theorised. Why is there not a regular size and spacing of settlements in Britain or any country you may wish to choose? Only in East Anglia where there is a greater degree of physical uniformity is there any approximation to a regular size and spacing of settlements.

The second way to view the urban system is as the product of a unique set of historical events which have produced the distribution of towns and cities in each country. Today that unique distribution of different sized places is the main recipient of government investment and assistance in order to steer the economic growth of the country. Governments do try to alter the nature of the urban system by controlling the growth of the largest cities as we have seen in Eastern Europe, by encouraging the development of new towns and cities and by assisting in the rebirth of the oldest parts of our largest cities as we shall see in Chapter 7.

Conclusion

Urbanisation is obviously a complex phenomenon which has produced a variety of urban systems. Perhaps to conclude you ought to ask yourself whether you can define the following key concepts starting with urbanisation and urban system. Here are some other key words and concepts which you can find used in the text:

city, conurbation, megalopolis, SMLA, cumulative causation, multiplier effect, rank-size rule, primate city, industrialisation, initial advantage, counterurbanisation, anti-urbanism, developed world, socialist world, communist world, third world.

Revision

1 Why is urbanisation a challenge for mankind?

2 What are the spatial, environmental and social impacts of urbanisation?

3 Is urbanisation a demographic, economic or social phenomenon?

2

The growth and structure of cities

The built expression of urbanisation has been the outward and upward growth of cities and the increasing segregation of functions within the city. How has the growth taken place? What explanations are there for growth following particular directions at periods in time? What impact has growth had on the present-day economic and social structure of cities? Can we actually see common elements in the structure of cities in Britain and elsewhere? What factors influence the pattern of land uses? These are the questions which we need to answer to provide us with an overview of the city before we move to a consideration of the individual elements of a city's structure.

Urban growth: Portsmouth

We have already seen in the case of Cardiff how the initial growth of the city took place around the old core along the routes leading to the pre-industrial inner city. On the whole most towns and cities show a concentric pattern of growth of the built-up area through time, that is unless other factors intervene to distort the pattern of growth from a purely concentric pattern.

If we examine the growth of a city such as Portsmouth (Figure 2.1) we can see how its growth has occurred. The original nucleus at the harbour mouth in Old Portsmouth was a walled, heavily defended town which rose to prominence after 1485 when the Royal Dockyard was created by Henry VII. In the seventeenth century the old town was overcrowded and development commenced near and in the dockyard in Portsea physically separated from the old town for military defence reasons. By the Napoleonic Wars the town had spread across to new areas north and east of the twin focii to form a ring of development housing the artisans in the northern area and the naval officers and well-to-do in the east in Southsea. Nineteenth century urbanisation mainly in the form of terraced rows spread in an increasingly wide arc, especially north along the main road into the city. Eastward spread in Southsea almost crossed the island although growth in the north-east was constrained by the railway line and the existence of major institutions such as hospitals and the prison.

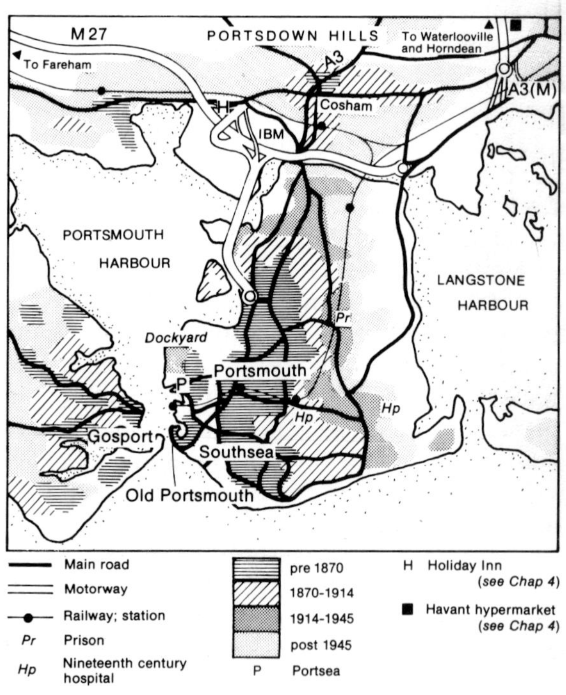

Figure 2.1 *The growth of Portsmouth*

A further ring of development took place on the island between 1914 and 1945; this over-spilled the island and spread out eastwards along the slopes of the Portsdown Hills which provide the backcloth to the city. Villa residences were also built in this period beyond the city along the main road towards London, encouraged by the opening of a tramway from within the city boundary at Cosham to Horndean. The post-war extensions to the built-up area within the **city region**, ie. that area served by and serving the city, took place in a discontinuous ring on the island, partly filling-up sites vacated by the military, and in major developments east and west of Cosham. Beyond these (off the map) a large housing area was built north of Havant at Leigh Park while the area fringing the A3 to London became one of the fastest expanding areas in Britain between 1950 and 1980. To the north west of the A3 large areas remained in agriculture. Meanwhile in the west and east, developments around former small towns such as Fareham and Emsworth have seen these towns almost submerged in the low density built-up area of the Portsmouth region. Villages both on other routes into the city, such as Waterlooville, and on the main railway lines have also experienced rapid expansion in the same period.

This brief sketch of Portsmouth's growth highlights several characteristics of the spread of an urban area.

(i) Growth is generally in a concentric form unless distorted.

(ii) Transport routes are a major element in structuring the growth of a city.

(iii) Important physical features such as a pronounced hill or, in this case, the coastline and marsh will steer growth in other directions.

(iv) Certain uses can repel development temporarily.

(v) Land owners such as the military or the private Southwick estate north-west of the city can withstand pressures for development, although the owners of Leigh Park did not do so.

(vi) This factor is not clear from our historical view, but the existence since 1947 of **town and country planning** has enabled the suburban areas to become more structured by controlling further sprawl and has encouraged the **infilling** of areas within the existing built-up area. On the whole the more recent the extensions to the built-up area the lower is the density of houses and population per hectare; a feature which we have already noted when we discussed counterurbanisation. We can now look at some of these factors in more detail selecting other towns and cities for the examples.

Study activity

1 Draw a sketch map to show the development of your own home town. To what extent has its growth been influenced by the six factors we have listed?
2 What differences do you notice between a map of growth of the built-up area and the age of buildings? Why have these differences occurred?

Urban growth and density

It was the demographer Colin Clark who first drew attention to the decline in density of population with distance from the city centre. He noted, as we can see in Figure 2.2a, that the densities declined very rapidly in the inner urban and middle distance suburbs and less rapidly in the outer suburbs of the more

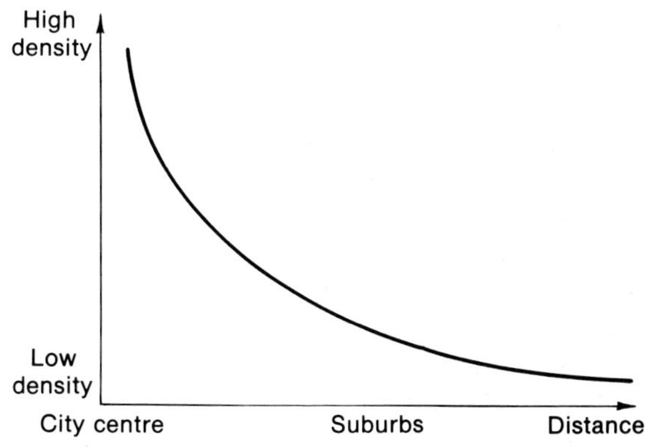

Figure 2.2a Negative exponential density curve

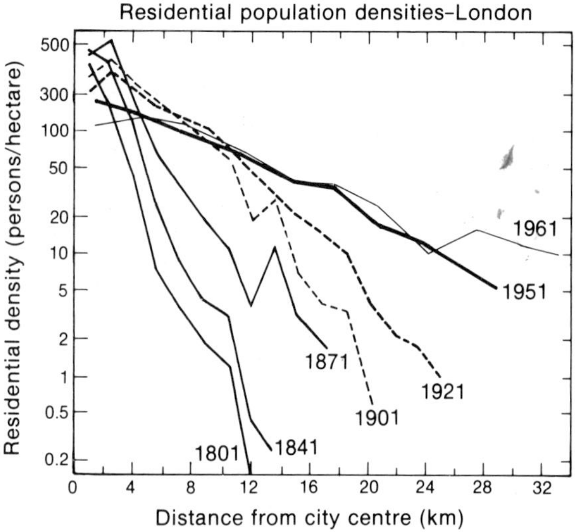

Figure 2.2b *Negative exonential density curves for London 1801–1961 plotted on semi-logarithmic graph paper*

recent past. This feature is called **the negative exponential density decline**. This concave density curve when plotted on semi-logarithmic graph paper assumes a straight line as in Figure 2.2b.

More interestingly developments since Clark wrote have shown that the negative exponential density curve has flattened over a twenty year period. This flattening is shown for London (Figure 2.2b), Toronto and Ottawa (Figure 2.2c). The pattern of curves for Ottawa illustrates a series of very normal declines in density with distance, the

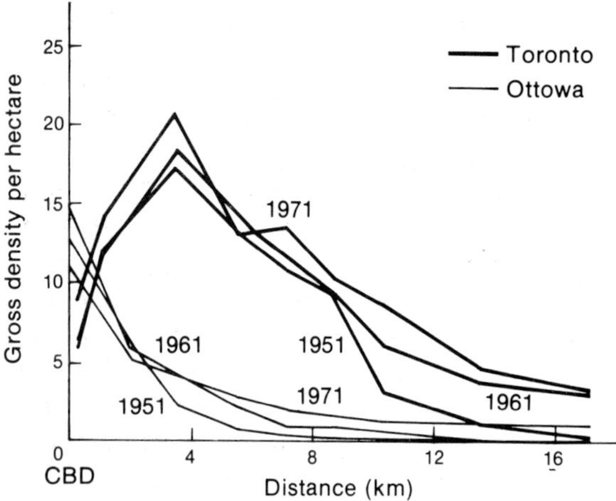

Figure 2.2c *Negative exponential density curve for Toronto and Ottawa, 1951–71*

rise in densities between 5 km and 18 km from the centre being the product of the affluent, space-buying desires among the growing population of Canada's capital city. In the case of Toronto the curve assumes what Yeates has termed an *'inverted lemon squeezer'* shape which probably reflects more accurately the pattern of most North American cities. There are low densities in the centre and the peak densities are beyond the central area and in the inner city. The familiar pattern of increasing densities in the outer suburbs is also present in these cases together with evidence of a rise in densities in the middle suburbs. In British and Western European cities there is a more pronounced rise in densities in the outer suburbs which is associated with the development in the last thirty years of **council housing** or **social housing** estates. This is similar to the high density squatter settlements in the third world. The resultant density curve is very much like that shown in Figure 2.3. Obviously if time of growth were the sole criterion then cities would assume an age-based concentric zonation similar to the simple model of **urban structure** developed by Burgess in 1920. No doubt you are familiar with Burgess' model.

Transport and city growth

The concentric ring model of city structure developed by Burgess failed to explain the impact of transport routes on city development. Without the developments in **transport**, the movement of people and goods, and **communications**, the movement of sound, ideas and knowledge, much city growth would have been slower. The evidence of the effects of transport is always more obvious in the larger cities such as London and reaches an extreme form in the cities of North America.

The pedestrian city was very compact and hence towns like Portsmouth were rarely very large in the late middle ages. Similarly until the Great Fire very little of London had spread beyond the square mile of the City of London. The horse was a luxury and so movement was on foot or by pulling goods in

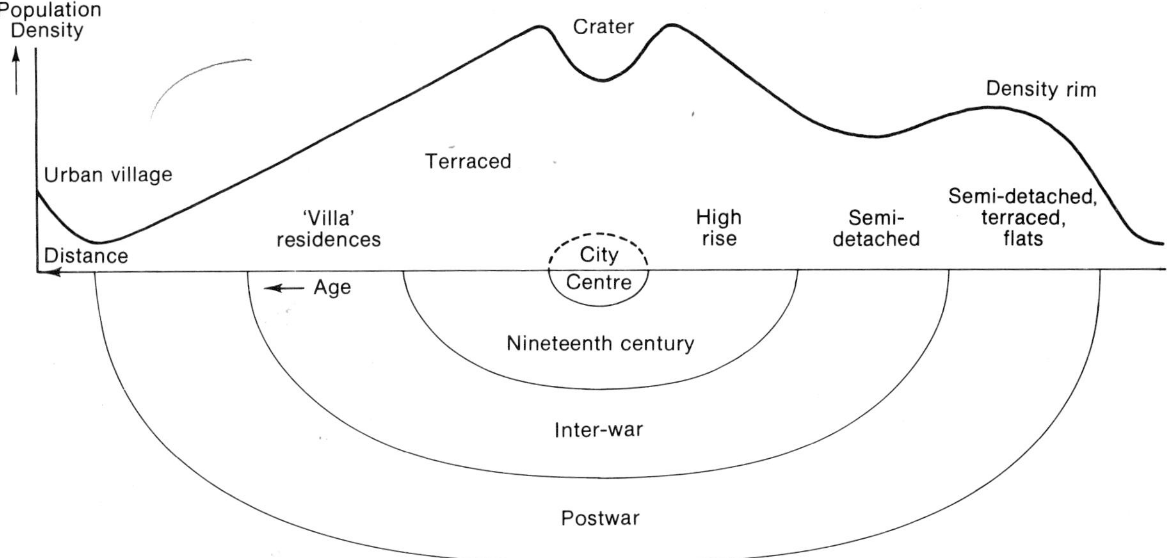

Figure 2.3 *The density curve with a high density rim*

carts. Some of the more privileged and wealthy were able to use the Thames as the main axis of movement as did royalty moving from Hampton Court to Westminster and the City. Not surprisingly some of the early seventeenth century expansion of London was in the form of large houses, such as Somerset House, located between the city and Westminster. In the eighteenth century the nobility and wealthy merchants were able to afford the costs of transport from the present West End area and the westward growth of that period was associated with the development of carriages. The turnpikes and the building of bridges upstream from London Bridge provided the incentive for the spread of London out across the floodplain terraces south of the city in the early nineteenth century. The improved roads aided the outward growth north of the Thames as well, both along the Oxford Road and out into the East End in Whitechapel.

The coming of the railway also produced a further spread to London along the routes of the new steam trains. The impact was variable but the railway and developments in railway technology have continued to have an effect on the growth of London. In the 1860s the development of the cheap working class return on the line to Enfield resulted in a corridor of late nineteenth century housing developments along the western side of the Lea valley. The rail network south of the Thames also resulted in rapid expansion of suburbs in the nineteenth century. Even in the inter-war period the railway companies and developers were working hand in hand to provide homes for the new middle income groups. Much of Ilford developed in this way as estate owners were persuaded to sell to the railway and developers. The electrification of the Southern Region sparked off urban growth south of London well into the North Downs especially down the Brighton line and in the semi-detached low density houses of Cheam and Raynes Park for example. In a similar way the underground and the later Tube lines which were built out to the green fields of Edgeware, Barnet and Cockfosters soon spawned large low density suburban townscapes. Hall has pointed out how in the 1930s the time distance of these new extensions to urban growth was about 45 minutes from the centre. More recently further improvements in rail travel brought about by electrification, diesel locomotives and the high speed train have meant that small towns and cities far beyond London have come within commuting distance and have expanded accordingly to house the long-distance commuter. Guildford, Horsham and, more impressively, Reading, only 30 minutes from London, have expanded since 1951. City workers now live in Bristol, Rugby and Cambridge. Rail has only had a major impact in the largest cities. In most European cities the tram and later bus routes had a similar stimulating effect on growth.

Study activity

1 Find out where the early tram and bus routes were in your town. Did they influence urban growth and if so, how?

In North America the railroads were not interested in urban lines because goods traffic brought in more money. Railroads only influenced the development of what have been termed **exurbs**; suburbs not physically joined to the rest of the city. Mont Royale in Montreal was one such railroad development. On the whole the major impact on city growth was the streetcar (trolley or tramcar) which was developed in the 1880s in response to the congestion of the horse omnibuses. The cable-car was an alternative in many cities although it only survives today in San Francisco as a tourist attraction. The impact of the streetcar on the growth of Toronto in the period after 1884 stands out very clearly as ribbons of development extending out beyond the built up area (Figure 2.4). The development of the streetcar system went hand in glove with land sales and speculation and gave rise to the term **streetcar suburbs**. Routes were laid out ahead of

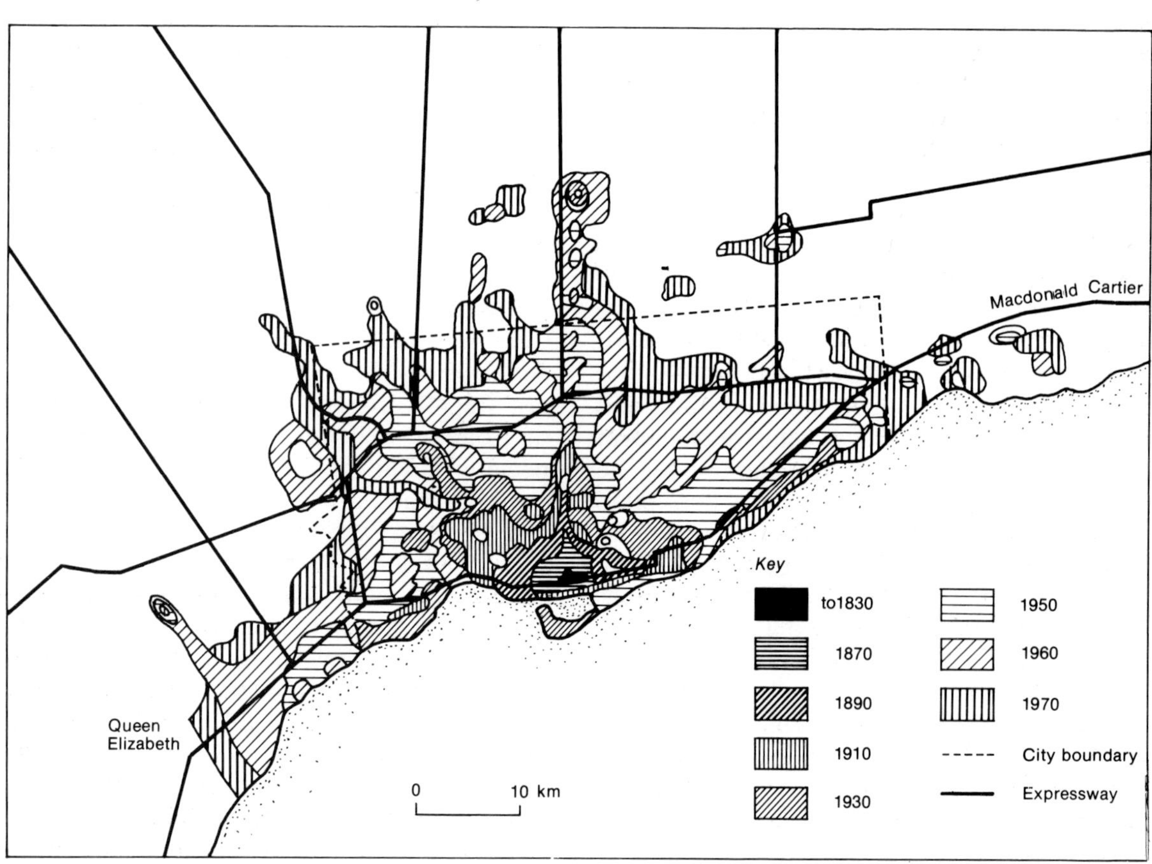

Figure 2.4 The growth of Toronto

urban growth which then followed as the developer and transit company linked up to build the homes for the middle classes.

It is in North America that the car has had the most dramatic impact on urban growth. Initially the car provided the means by which the areas between the streetcar suburbs were developed slowly. However, the building of the freeways in the intervening gaps both acted as a stimulus to development near the city and subsequently it provided the ready access to the city for the mid-twentieth century suburbanites who could now live even further afield. The effects of freeways such as the Macdonald Cartier, and Queen Elizabeth around Toronto can be seen in the expansion of the urbanised area since 1960. In the case of Toronto there have been two developments more recently which parallel European developments. First, the development in 1967 of Go-Transit commuting from nearby towns such as Oshawa is acting as a catalyst for east-west spread. Second, Air Atonabee provides morning and evening commuter plane services to Peterborough and Ottawa (135km and 400km distant respectively). In a much more minor way the aeroplane is having a similar effect to the Intercity 125 route to Bristol. Transport growth which seems to move in cycles of innovation and development followed by surges in building therefore distorts the concentric pattern of growth (Figure 2.4).

The impact of transport is not solely on growth. It has an impact on structure which we will consider separately.

Physical geography and development

In the case of Portsmouth we have already seen the barrier effect of the Portsdown Hills. Most prominent relief features whether they are steep hills, marked gullies or ravines will tend to prevent the spread of development. The growth of Paris in the early twentieth century illustrates the way that the plateau areas which penetrate towards the Seine valley, were not developed for a long time, partly because the transport lines followed the valleys which penetrated the plateau. Rivers can act as a barrier to growth on the opposite bank until more bridges are built. The limited number of crossing points over the Thames at Reading has restricted growth in the Caversham area. Similarly the limited crossings over the Danube in Vienna have had the same effect.

River valleys have provided the corridors of growth in the South Wales valleys with very little development taking place on the interfluves until recent times. In Trier and Wuppertal the city has spread up and down the Mosel and Wupper valley respectively and a little up the sides but only recently has growth really spilled up out of the valleys. This is understandable because building costs and the provision of water and sewage disposal rise dramatically if there are marked variations in relief; it is more costly in time and energy to develop up the valley sides rather than along the valley floor.

Waterfronts and seafronts have usually acted as a stimulus to growth. Figure 2.4 shows how development in Toronto spread along the Ontario lakeshore. The seafronts of most English seaside resorts show a similar early breadth of development from the centre and pierhead with relatively little inland depth.

Study activity

How have physical features affected the growth of a town or city known to you?

Planning and city growth

In the last thirty years in Britain the outward spread of cities has been slowed down through the more judicious allocation and control over land released for development. So far as growth is concerned the main effects of planning have been to control the spread of the city by the creation of **green belts**, zones of open land from which most urban development is prohibited. The designation of limits to urban growth in a particular direction embodied in local policies is

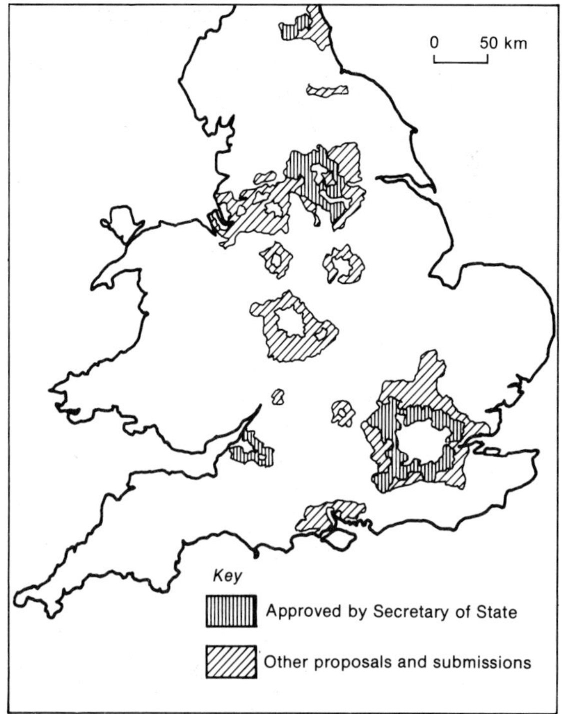

Figure 2.5 Green belts in England and Wales

another way in which the planner makes an impact. Conversely by encouraging the release of land for development in another area the structure of the city will be altered.

In Britain the designation of green belts originates from an Act of Parliament in 1938 and the first green belt was completed around London in 1955 (Figure 2.5). Since that time green belts have been established around other cities. (See Chapter 6.) A final unique case of public control is that of Saskatoon (Figure 2.6). Here land has been forfeited to the city by people unable to pay their local taxes and to this land has been added purchases made by the city, the provincial and federal government so that the local authority controls much of the rural fringe to the city. As a result, land speculation is unable to take place close to the city and the city is able to control the development of the suburbs. In this case government intervention and ownership have controlled the growth of Saskatoon. The Community Land Act 1975 had similar intentions here in

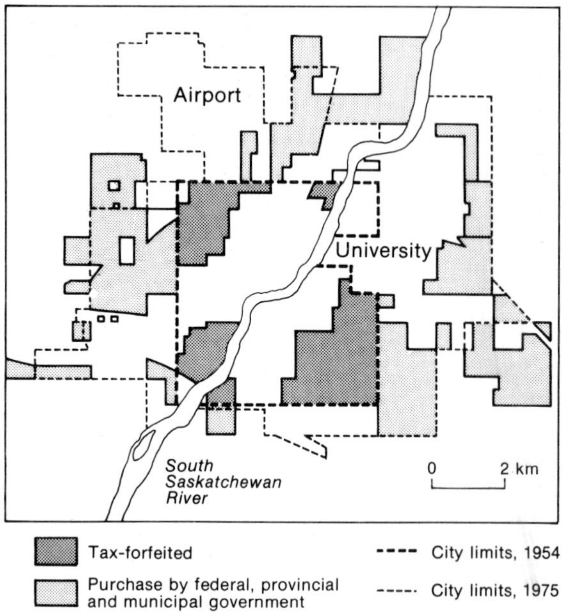

Figure 2.6 Forfeited land around Saskatoon

Britain but it has since been abandoned.

Study activity

What controls exist over the future use and direction of development around your home town or a town which you have studied in the field or on maps?

The internal structure of cities

So far we have concerned ourselves merely with the growth of towns which is obviously one major element in the **structure**, the arrangement of land uses or functions within the city. Generally new developments are to be found nearer the edge of the city unless **redevelopment** has taken place in the older districts. (This topic will be covered in Chapter 4.) Given the constraints which we have covered, growth will provide a concentric accumulation of housing areas, factory types and types of shopping facilities which are typical of the time the area was developed. For instance, the **corner shop** in the nineteenth century terraces, the **shopping arcade** in inter-war and post-war developments and more recently the **precinct** and **hypermarket** in the new suburbs and beyond, illustrate the sequence of retailing developments in both time and space. A similar concentric zonation is frequently assumed for the age of the inhabitants. The typical view is that the inhabitants of the inner areas are older on average than those of the new suburbs on the fringes where families are more likely to be concentrated.

Others have tried to show that the functional areas of cities are arranged in **sectors**. Notable among these was Hoyt who in 1939 proposed a sectoral arrangement to the city's structure. If we examine British cities there are definite sectors of a similar type of function which have developed from core areas close to the centre. Part of the sectoral arrangement is the product of transport with industrial areas grouping along the main routes in and out of a city. Thus in Bath the industrial area is a sector which has grown west from the centre along the Avon valley. Sectors have been readily recognised in terms of the better and less prosperous sides of a town. West Sheffield is a more desirable residential address than the east. South west London is preferred whereas the east is not. Hoyt in particular noted the very marked sectoral shape of the areas inhabited by the most wealthy, the upper middle class in North American cities. In London the sector south-west from Putney, Richmond, Kingston, out to Camberley and Ascot is very well defined. In Southampton the sector developed northwards from the centre, along The Avenue (a broad park lined road) to the Bassett area where the University is located and beyond to Chandler's Ford (Figure 2.7). There is a similar sector in Edinburgh (Figure 2.7) stretching west from the Georgian New Town to Crammond the right place to be even at the time of *The Prime of Miss Jean Brodie*. In Paris it is the west of the city, the XVIth arrondissement, St Cloud and out to Versailles that contains the highest proportions of the upper social groups (Figure 2.7). Similar sectors can be located in Hamburg or in Bulawayo where the area north of the town is the best sector and is neatly cut off by the rail tracks from the sector containing the African townships and the main industrial areas.

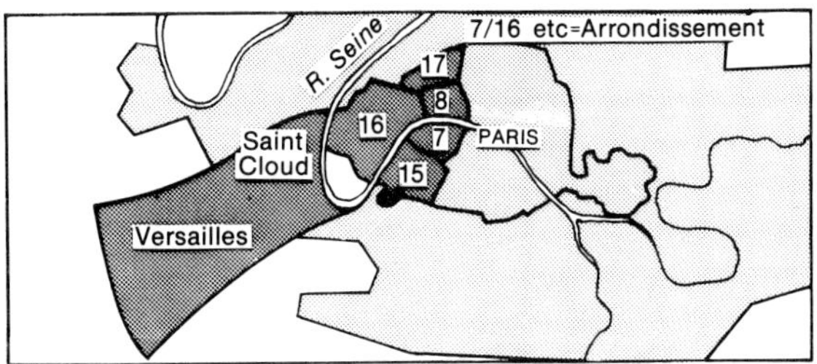

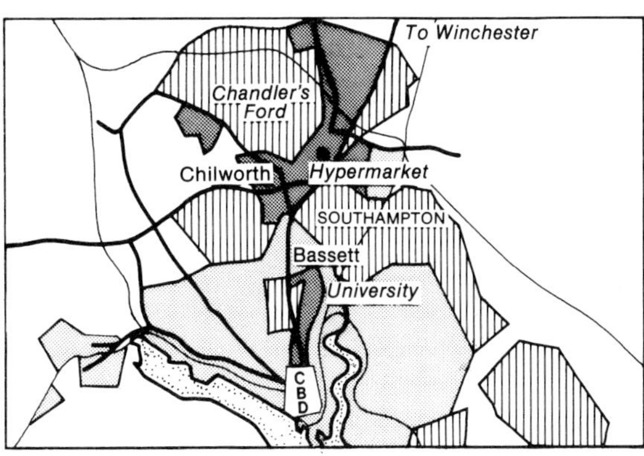

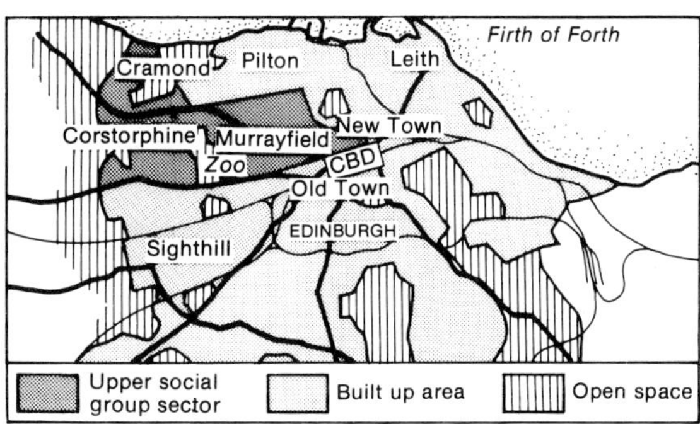

Figure 2.7 Upper socio-economic group sectors in Paris, Southampton and Edinburgh

There is evidence therefore that the structure of the city is a complex interplay between concentric rings and sectors. This has been stressed both in Britain and Canada. Mann in his model of the British city

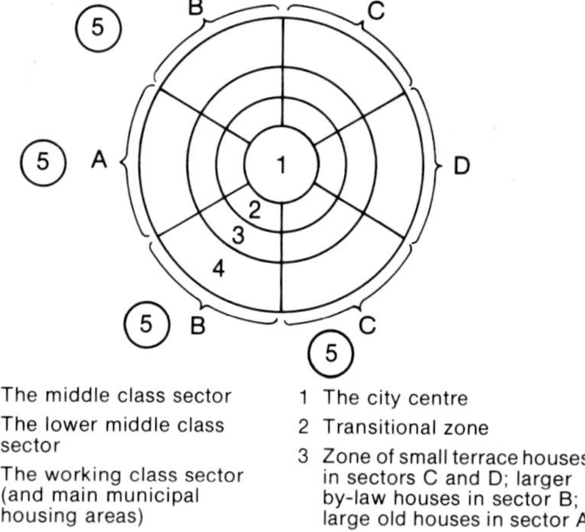

Figure 2.8 Mann's model of the British city

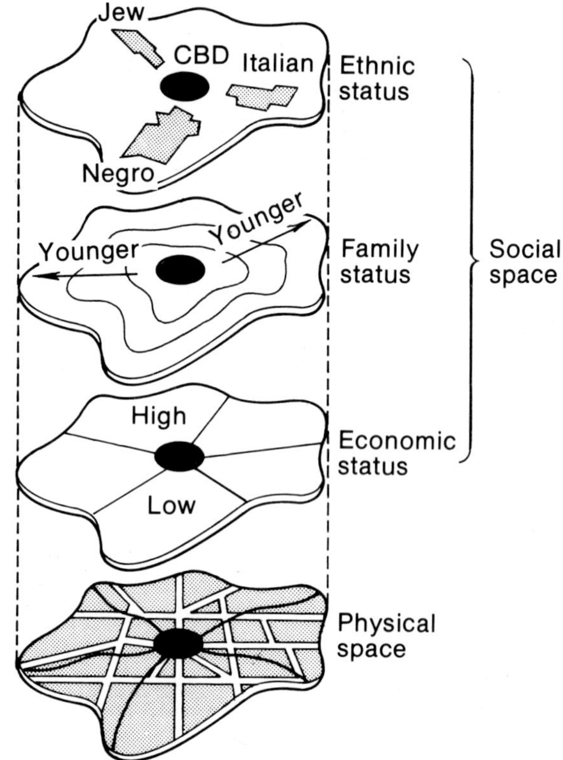

Figure 2.9 Murdie's three types of space in Toronto

devised a complex relationship (Figure 2.8) on the basis of a study of north British towns. In many ways his patterns are the summation of the ideas expressed by Murdie in his model of the three types of space in Toronto (Figure 2.9). On **physical space** we have seen the imprint of **social space** which has a concentric zonation and upon this we have **economic space** (including wealth) which has a sectoral pattern. It is this self-same interlinking that underpins Robson's model of the British city (Figure 2.10).

Two other factors which we have yet to consider in fashioning the structure of cities must be added at this point. The first is that of land values and the second, governmental activity.

Land values and city structure

It was Alonso who noted that the rents for urban land resembled that of rural land developed by Von Thünen. The rents that users are prepared to pay generally declines with distance from the city centre. The city centre has certain **positional advantages** in terms of accessibility to the whole city and convenience as a meeting place for a large number of people. Therefore as Figure 2.11 shows, offices, banks and retailing are prepared to pay highly for central sites. This type of diagram, the **bid-rent diagram** has been modified by Bunge to suggest the location of the rich and poor areas of town because the higher the cost of land, the greater the rent or price and therefore the higher the density of housing for the land to be profitable (Figure 2.12a).

However, **bid-rents** (the price one is prepared to pay) are based on the land values and not building values. Older buildings may not be as useful as new ones and therefore the land values for the sites may actually be lower. In fact the curve of land values probably shows a series of peaks (Figure 2.12b) coinciding with the points of greater accessibility in the suburbs and around the city fringes where a by-pass traverses a major route leading into the city. The overall land value surface in three dimensions thus re-

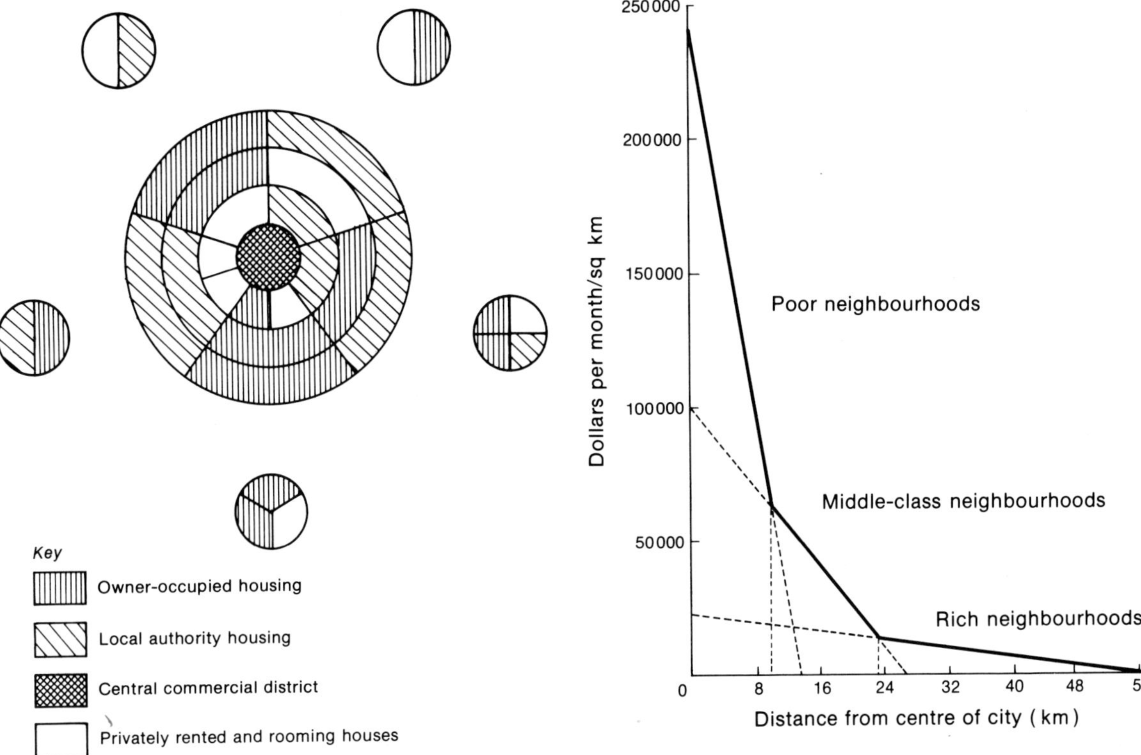

Figure 2.10 Robson's model of the British city

Figure 2.12a Modification of the bid-rent curve by Bunge for housing areas

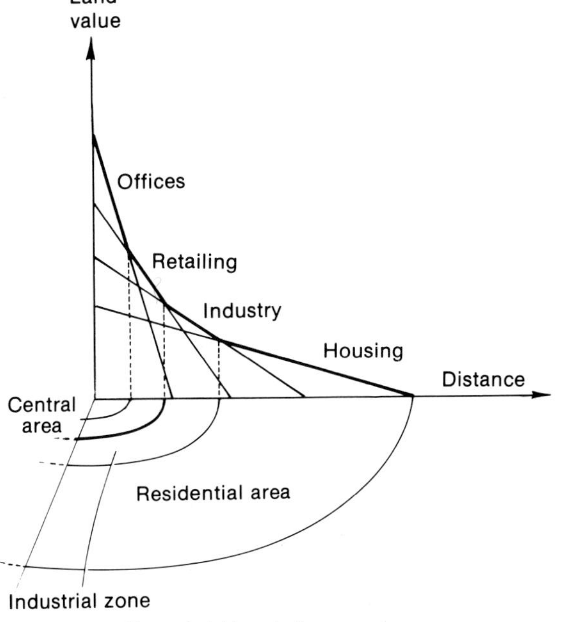

Figure 2.11 Alonso's bid-rent diagram

sembles a spider's web raised at the centre and with a series of peaks in the outer mesh.

Government and city structure

The impact of government is best illustrated in Britain by the development of council housing. The location of council housing in Sunderland for instance is peripheral on land where the purchase costs were low. Developed at high density this then gives the

Study activity

1 Draw your own approximate land value surface for your home town. How closely does it resemble the models used here?
2 Why is it difficult to construct a land value surface for a town? What source of data would aid the completion of the map?

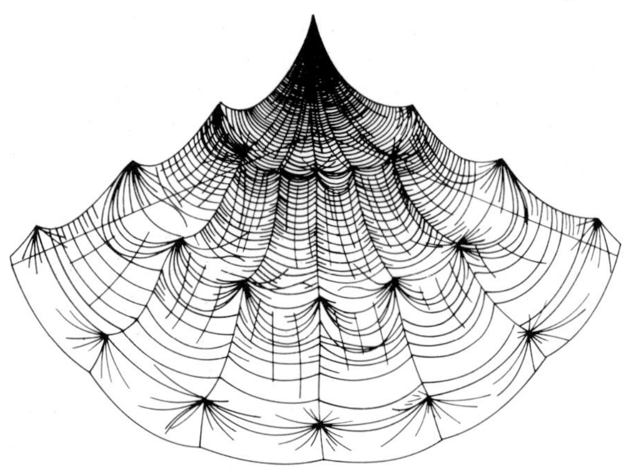

Figure 2.12b Multiple peaked land-value surface after Garner

governmental purchasers a relatively high return in rents. Similar peripheral council housing developments can be found in almost all cities: Coventry's Bell Green; Edinburgh at Sighthill, Pilton and Craigmillar; and Bristol's Bedminster; are other British examples. Similar developments have been common in Western Europe such as Neu Perlach, Munich, Sarcelles north of Paris, Sloetermeer outside Amsterdam and Gropiusstadt, West Berlin.

Land use zoning, the allocation of a particular land use or combination of functions to an area, is a further way in which governments have been able to influence the overall structure of the city. In Britain the legal foundations for zoning were introduced in the 1947 Town and Country Planning Act which was updated in 1968 and modified in 1980 (see chapter 6). Most developed countries have some form of zoning controls to prevent the juxtaposition of incompatible uses or the destruction of the character of an area by changes of use. Thus in some cities the planners have acted to prevent the conversion of shops into building society's offices which would radically alter the existing character of an established shopping street. Industry and warehousing have been segregated into distinct estates. Controls exist over the density of housing whether it be 3.2(8), 4.0(10) or 5.6(14) per hectare (acre) with the result that the social groups who inhabit an area are obviously those who can afford the mortgage costs of a larger or smaller house and plot. Density can also be controlled by height regulations such as those that exist in central Paris or by controls on the ratio of floor area to the plot size. Both of these measures can result in the spread of the central area. In other cases planners may place conditions on developments that have further ramifications such as the controls on the acceptable type of building stone which exist in Bath and the Cotswold towns.

Structure models of cities

We have already noted the way in which the distribution of economic activities and social groups in British cities varies from the models derived from North American studies. In fact the more that we examine cities the more each nation or cultural area of a continent seems to have led to the development of a distinctive city structure.

Studies in Western Europe show a strong resemblance to the British case. Much is probably due to the strong historic legacy which has made the city centre a distinctive entity worthy of preservation from the worst ravages of the developer. Newer office districts have therefore grown up just outside the centre. New social housing areas on the periphery, as we have already noted, have added a further distinctive element. A third element has been the strength of inner urban industrial areas which are often associated with a river port or some other major transport area. This can all be seen in Figure 2.13 which is a combination of several models of the Western European city.

Wreford-Watson has recently provided us with an interesting updated structure model of the American city (Figure 2.14) which is very much based on a combination of land values and accessibility. However, it ignores aspects of social geography, particularly the concentration of ethnic minorities into distinct areas. Like the models of Burgess, Hoyt and Mann this seems to be a product of its time ie the 1970s.

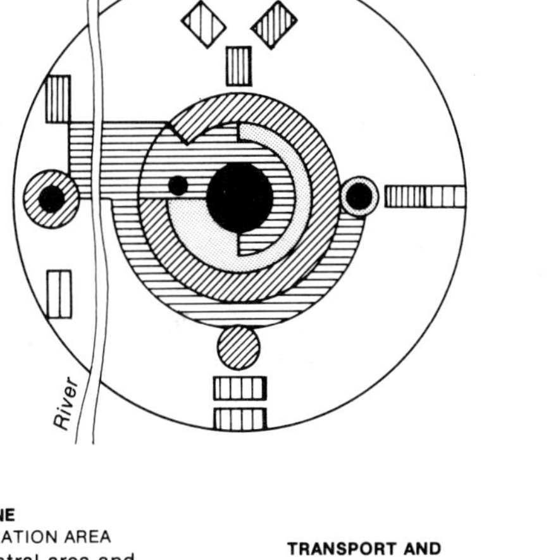

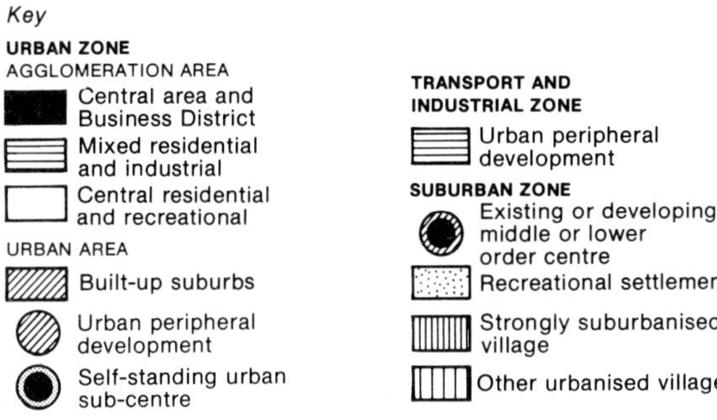

Figure 2.13 Nellner's model of the Western European city

In the Socialist cities of Eastern Europe and the Soviet Union where, in theory, all land is nationalised and where there is centralised planning, there is much more scope for the state to influence the structure of the city. Nevertheless the studies which do exist do show that, despite attempts to lessen the social divisions, there is still a distinct structure to the city. Hamilton has shown that the pre-1945 city with its old core and business area is surrounded by the housing areas of the pre-1945 social groups. Since 1945 new socialist housing areas and large industrial zones around the green belt surrounding the city have been developed along with a new city centre and other nodes in the new pattern of life of the inhabitants (Figure 2.15). Thus the city structure is a blend of the older very distinctive early city with the more uniform socialist city.

Very recently satellite photography has been used to assist geographers who have been trying to look at the urban structure of Chinese cities. Peking (Beijing) was to become a model socialist city and Landsat photographs taken in 1978 reveal the model city to have distinct areas based on the density of buildings (Figure 2.16). The old pre-revolution walled city forms the innermost zone which also contains the Forbidden City, large public buildings and assembly areas such as Tian An Men Square (Peoples' Square). The more recently developed zone contains more new residential areas built at a lower density besides new pollution-free factories, offices and universities. The outer zone includes **satellite towns** such as Shijingshan and Fengtai, suburbs, and offices intermixed with intensively used market gardens.

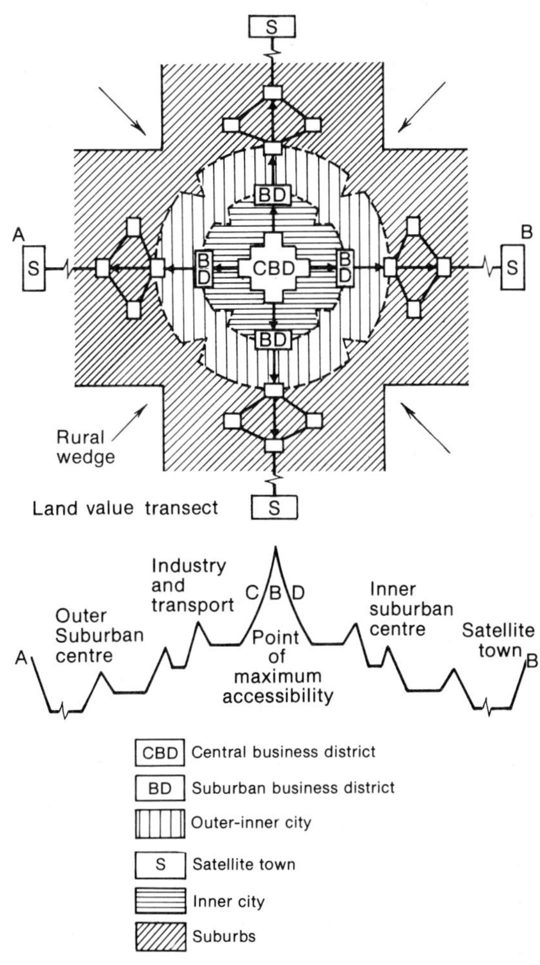

Figure 2.14 Wreford-Watson's North American city

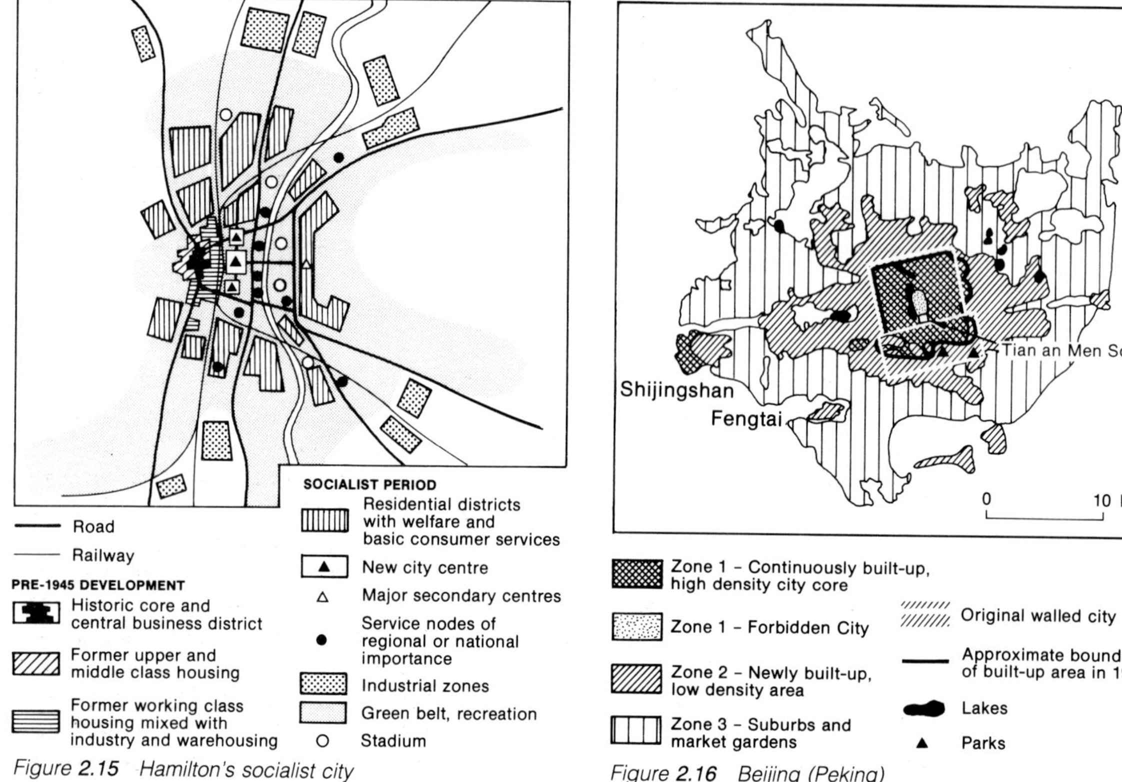

Figure 2.15 *Hamilton's socialist city*

Figure 2.16 *Beijing (Peking)*

Conclusion

The growth and structure of cities shows considerable variations throughout the world. Nevertheless one can identify common processes at work even if the resultant structures are distinct. The roles of history, culture, physical geography, transport, land values, planning and government have been stressed in this chapter. The role of social factors has been touched upon and we will return to these in Chapter 5.

Study activity

See if you can find maps of the economic and social regions of other cities. Can you explain why they vary from those which have been outlined?

Revision

1 What factors have caused the structure of cities to vary from one region to another?
2 By reference to your home town assess the contribution of the six factors influencing a town's growth.
3 Define the following:
(a) negative exponential density decline
(b) exurbs and suburbs
(c) precint.
4 Distinguish physical, social and economic space.
5 With what ideas and concepts do you associate the following authors: H Hoyt; Mann; W Alonso; F E I Hamilton; Burgess; W Bunge?

3
The city centre

The city centre is the focus of urban life and, in much of the world, the economic heart of a city. It is made up of a whole series of activities. Shops and offices are the two major users but as we shall see there are others, such as administration, education, recreation and tourism. The city centre is frequently located in (or partly in) the historic centre of the town which contains many physical components of a city's heritage which give the city identity and character such as a castle, a market or a cathedral. So the **central area** is an area of considerable variety of land-users both horizontally and vertically, and the **central business district** or **CBD** is the more confined area of retailing and offices which has expanded and changed in character over the past century. Change in the city centre has brought in its wake a set of problems and we will examine the difficulties which change has produced in recent years.

Central areas in Newcastle-upon-Tyne and Chichester

Newcastle-upon-Tyne is the main city serving the north-east of England and its centre might be regarded as a typical example of a large city centre in Britain. The present day central area has spread north from the medieval focus on the north bank of the river Tyne (Figure 3.1). **Retailing** has become concentrated at the heart or **core** of the CBD within the area bounded by Percy Street, Newgate Street, Grainger Street and Northumberland Street with a modern focus being the covered Eldon Square shopping centre. Offices have concentrated south of the retailing district especially along Collingwood Street and Grey Street and occasionally above some of the shops in the area. There is a large modern extension to the office core in the All Saints area straddling the ring motorway (Figure 3.1). Surrounding the CBD are a series of other **central functions**. In the north-west there is a large area devoted to the Royal Victoria Infirmary and the University and its halls of residence, which include some preserved Georgian terraces. The Civic Centre and City Hall separate the University campus from that of the Polytechnic. Beyond these the urban motorway ring and Town Moor provides a strong northern boundary.

The edges of the central area or **frame** are more blurred elsewhere, although they are dominated by transport uses such as the Central Station, the Marlborough Crescent bus station, assorted ground level car parks and second-hand car sales areas. In the same south-western corner there are some printing works and various business services. Between the station and the Tyne is an area of former wholesaling and industry which is undergoing renovation. Similarly, between the All Saints offices and the Quayside is another area of conserved buildings now undergoing renovation. It is hoped that this area will become a focus of tourism and recreation once new uses can be found for the buildings. Newcastle has no hotel district although there are several major hotels within the central area.

Chichester is a much smaller city centre serving the West Sussex coastal area. Here the central area is still confined within the Roman Walls and includes several large residential areas, and a well defined ecclesi-

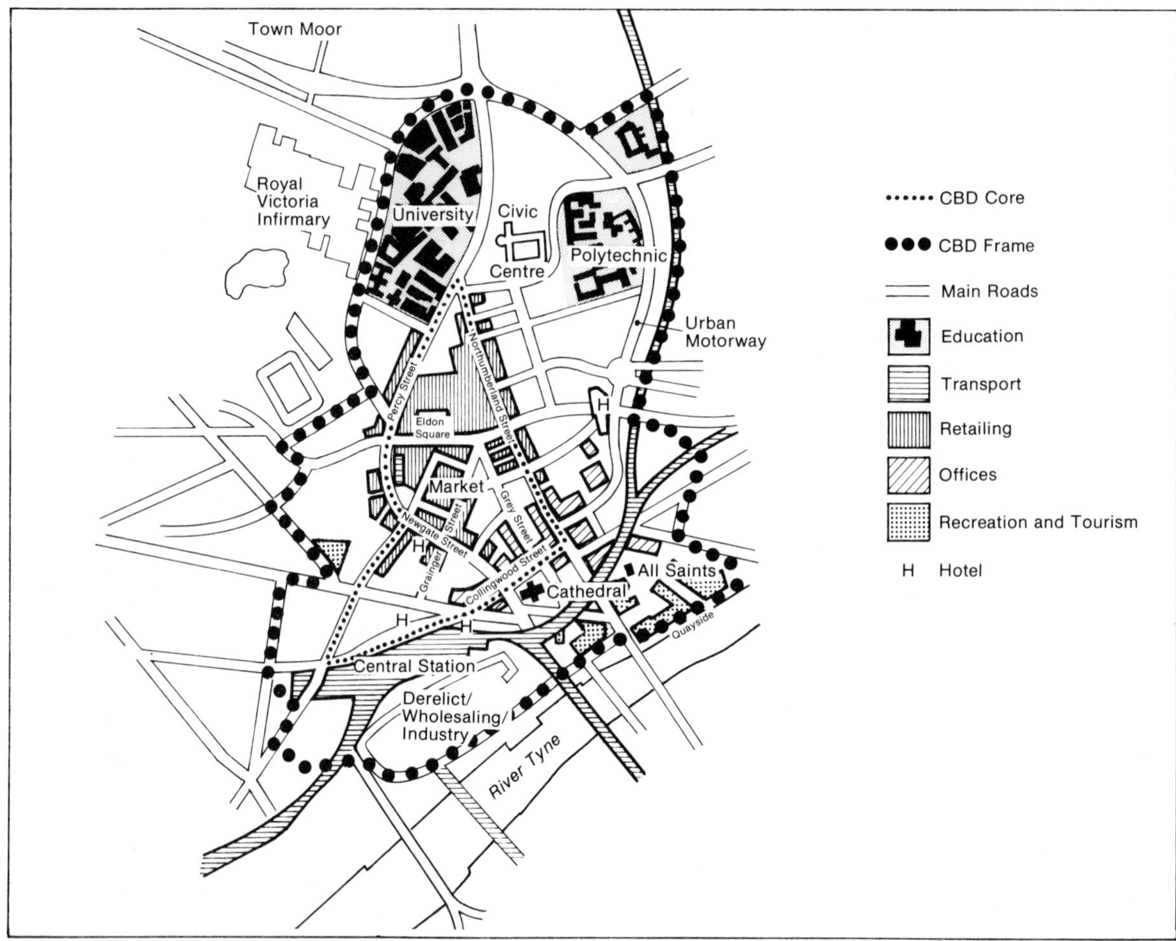

Figure 3.1 The central area of Newcastle-upon-Tyne

astical precinct surrounding the Norman cathedral in the south-west quadrant (Figure 3.2). Retailing is almost entirely confined to the North Street–South Street axis and an extension along East Street with storage offices or vacant space in the upper storeys. County administration is concentrated in the north-west quarter and other local administration and private offices are found in the conservation area of The Pallants. Surrounding this core there are car parks, an industrial function and beyond the walls, the thriving agricultural market. Hotels and restaurants abound but the cinema has closed and the Festival Theatre and the relatively minor educational campuses are well beyond the centre.

These two cities serve to illustrate several points concerning the central area of cities. First, the nature of the central area varies with the size of city. The larger the population of the city and its region or **hinterland**, the more varied are the functions that can be found. The larger the population the easier it is for various **threshold populations**, ie. the number of people needed to support a function, to be exceeded. Chichester can only support one small **department store** whereas there are two in Newcastle. Second there are specialist areas both within retailing and offices in Newcastle which are much more identifiable both from the quality and the types of the goods and services. This is less so in Chichester.

Obviously in the largest cities the central area functions become more spatially

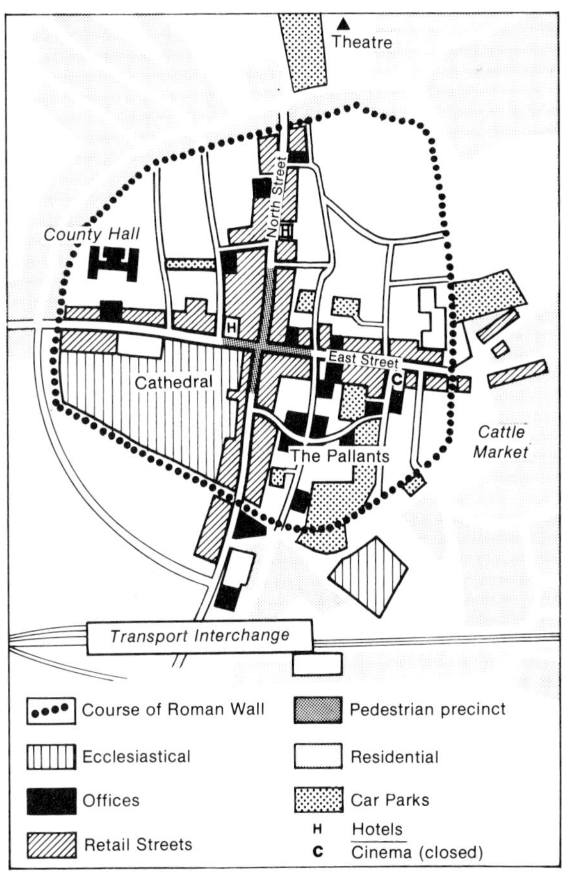

Figure 3.2 The central area of Chichester

segregated and specialised. Thus in London, offices are traditionally concentrated in the city but these are mainly concerned with banking, finance and insurance, all of which have their distinct quarters. Entertainment is concentrated in the West End and ranges from the theatres to the sleazy back street sex shops and cinema clubs of the Soho area. Very marked specialisms have developed in retailing as well. At the general level there is the distinction between popular Oxford Street where the north and south facing sides are very distinct and fashionable Bond Street. At the specialised level there is a concentration of Hi-Fi retailing in Tottenham Court Road, the popular fashions in Oxford Street and high quality tailoring in Savile Row.

Although the central area can be defined by land use at the ground floor level and both above and below ground, it has been identified in other ways. As we saw in the bid-rent model it is the area of highest land values. Therefore one can use land or building values as a guide to the extent of the area. But these values are hard to find because sales in the central area are rare and so, in Britain, it might be better to take the rateable value of each property and relate that to each metre of street frontage. This will give front/metre values. Then with all the values plotted it is possible to decide the limits of the central area. Another method that has been used is to work out the ratio of ground floor in a street block to the total area of central business district uses for that block. The **central business height index** was devised in the USA hence the use of street blocks which are of uniform size there. A further measure used in the USA is the **central business intensity index** which divides the total floor area devoted to central business uses in a block by the total floor area of the street block. Once again the higher the value the nearer you are to the core. In both cases arbitrarily chosen values would mark the edge of the central area. A final characteristic is that the central area has a high day-time population and a low night-time population although this is more difficult to measure.

The central area's size and degree of specialisation is a function of the city's place in the urban hierarchy which we outlined in Chapter 1. It is an area of intensive land use and increased vertical scale in larger centres. It is obviously a major focus of employment with the larger centres being more dependent on public transport. London has a well-developed public transport system and the Tyne and Wear Metro opened in 1980 has improved public transport access to Newcastle. Chichester's workers and shoppers arrive predominantly by car and on foot. Finally, the shape of the central area varies with relief and other major barriers to spread such as parks, old buildings, motorways and railway lines.

Study activity

1 Figure 3.3 shows a typical CBD of a North American city. What size of city is the author using? What might he mean by Skid Row? Do British cities have such an area?
2 Draw a sketch map of the central area of a town or city known to you. Mark the areas of retailing, offices, entertainment and conservation. Can you identify a core to the area and a frame area beyond that? (This activity would form a useful exercise during a field class.)

City centre retailing

The shops in a city centre cater both for the inhabitants of the area, few though they might be, and those from near and far who use the centre with varying frequency. There are also variations in the quality of the product sold and the types of shop from which goods are sold. All these variables are present in the changing retail centre of the city. Certain types of function do appear to concentrate and it is possible to measure the degree of clustering. On the whole clusters are found where the consumer wishes to compare the goods' quality and price. Shoe shops and clothing shops are **comparison goods** outlets that tend to exhibit clustering. Similarly the major **chain** or **variety stores** such as Marks and Spencer, BHS, C & A, Littlewoods, Boots and W H Smith also cluster because they rely on visitors coming to a centre to purchase goods from several outlets. All these outlets prefer to be located on pedestrian precincts or in purpose-built centres such as Newcastle's Eldon Square, Nottingham's Victoria Centre or the Whitgift Centre in Croydon.

Banks, building societies and other banking, finance and loan shops have also shown a distinct preference to cluster in parts of the retailing area and, very frequently, at the very heart of the city. The preference of banks and building societies for locations in and close to the area of highest land values, outbidding the traditional retailers, has become a major concern for city planning authorities. This sector is what some people now call the **quasi-retail sector** because they are not shops and not really offices. Where clusters have occurred they have been banned from the major retailing streets by policies laid down by the city council.

Food retailing is less common in the larger city centres although supermarkets can be found usually around the edge of the retailing district and preferably close to car parks. The exceptions are the traditional markets such as Grainger Markets in Newcastle which still contains Marks and Spencer's original Penny Bazaar and the specialist, quality delicatessen. However, in a centre the size of Chichester food retailing is scattered along the main streets.

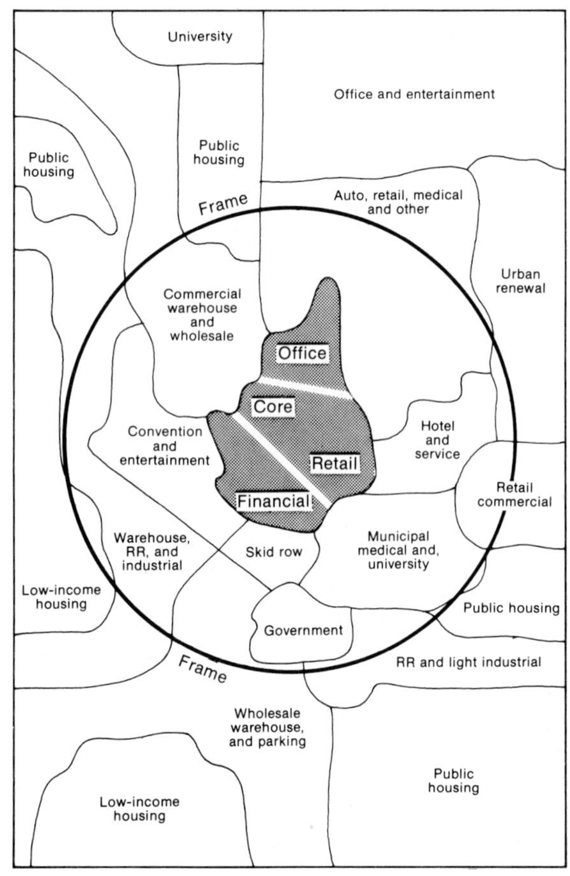

Figure 3.3 *Functional areas of a hypothetical North American CBD (after Hartshorne)*

Study Activity
Nearest Neighbour Analysis

1 On an appropriate map of your city centre (ie. 1:10000) locate the shoe and clothing shops or any other category that you wish.
2 Measure the area of the shopping centre in square metres = A.
3 Calculate the distance in metres of all shoe shops (for example) from one another and divide by the total number (n) of shoe shops to obtain the mean distance = $\bar{d}_o$ the observed distance.
NB: Distance and area measures must be in the same units.
4 Calculate the expected distance

$$\bar{d}_e = \frac{1}{2\sqrt{\frac{n}{A}}}$$

ie. ½ × the square root of the number of shoe shops divided by the area (step 2).
5 The nearest neighbour measure $R_n = \frac{\bar{d}_o}{\bar{d}_e}$
ie. divide the answer from step 3 by the answer of step 4.
6 The answer will be somewhere on a scale from 0 to 2.1491. The nearer to 0 your answer the greater the degree of clustering of the shops with a figure of 1.0 indicating a random pattern of shops.
7 Attempt to explain why some patterns are clustered in your city.

Changing central area retailing

We are already aware of new types of retailing areas such as the pedestrian precinct and the shopping centre which are increasingly common in city centres today. As the population has settled further from the city centre the shopping areas have had to become both more accessible to the suburban dweller and more attractive than centres in the suburbs, otherwise a decline of city centre shopping might ensue. Decline has occurred in city centre shopping most dramatically in the USA. For instance hardly a shop or store remains in central San José, California, now that most have transferred their business to suburban covered shopping **malls** such as the Eastridge Centre. In Britain and Western Europe local authorities and property developers have striven to keep the city centre as the main shopping area of town.

The **pedestrianisation** of the city centre, or at least a part of it, to provide a **traffic free zone** was first used in Stevenage new town and has spread to almost every town and city. Pedestrian areas have often existed in the market areas such as the Grainger Markets (Newcastle) but the removal of the noise and fumes from traffic, and the building of a landscaped street with plants, and seats has often enhanced the trade of shops. A pedestrian precinct does require rear delivery space for the shops or alternatively permission for deliveries to take place at certain times. This latter method is used in many West German cities. Precincts also necessitate the moving of bus routes to adjacent streets although it is possible to permit buses and taxis only along a street as in Cornmarket Street, Oxford and Northumberland Street, Newcastle. In Hannover, the city trams still pass along the pedestrianised main shopping street so encouraging the use of public transport and favouring the non-car owning population. In some cases it is im-

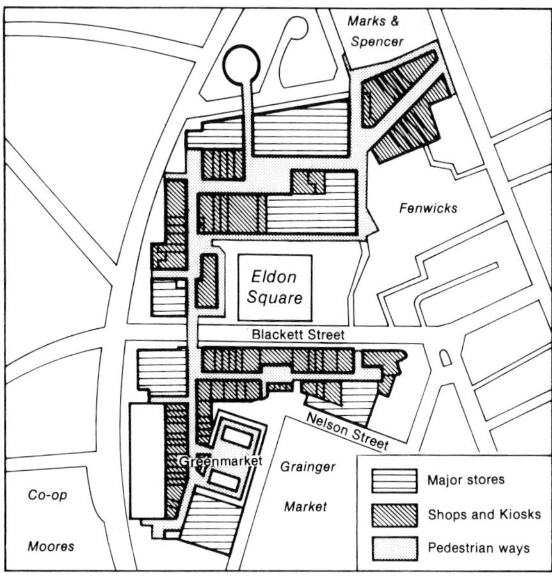

Figure 3.4 Eldon Square, Newcastle-upon-Tyne

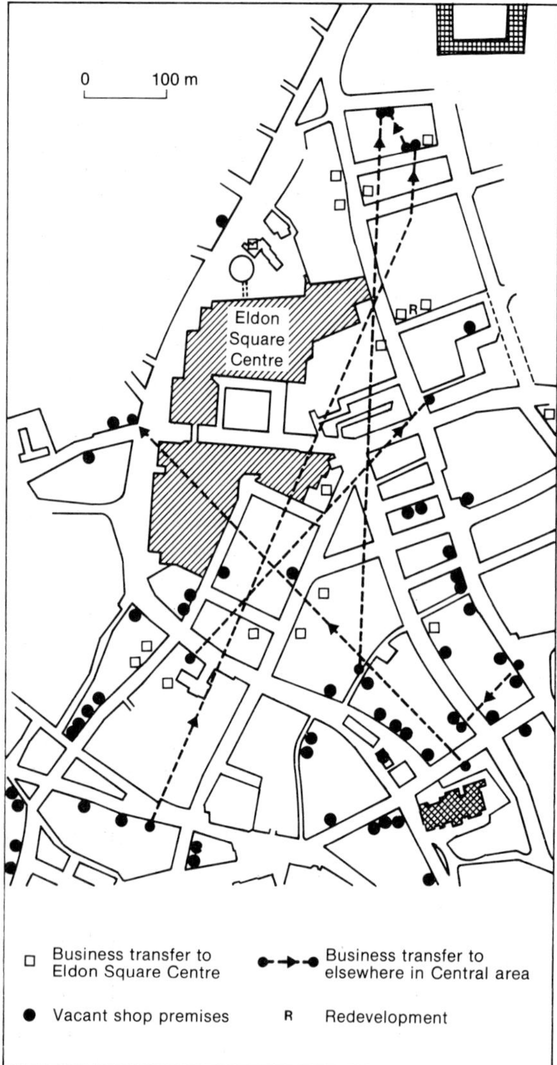

Figure 3.5 Shop movements into Eldon Square

possible to pedestrianise because alternative traffic routes do not exist. In Ottawa, Bank Street has been kept open to traffic but the pedestrian area now fills half the street prohibiting on-street parking but improving the environment for pedesrian shopping.

More importantly in the last twenty years purpose-built shopping centres have been opened in many city centres such as Eldon Square, Newcastle (Figure 3.4), and the Arndale and Exchange Centres in Manchester. Today, these centres with their air-conditioned environment and a layout deliberately determined by the developer to encourage the shopper into the scheme are an important asset for the city centre. The 120 shop units in Eldon Square attracted not only the major national chains but also other shops, such as the Bainbridges department store, from other parts of Newcastle (Figure 3.5). It is also sited above a station on the Tyne and Wear Metro and has an integrated bus station and two multistorey car parks for 1700 cars. Eldon Square also has a large recreation complex on its third floor. One of the problems caused by such a centre has been the decline of the retailing in other parts of the centre. Bainbridges' old premises took time to re-let and Clayton Street and Newgate Street had many vacancies. Older shops more distant from the new centre have been the most difficult to re-let although gradually more specialised traders have moved in.

Study question

1 What are the main advantages and disadvantages of a major change in the shopping area of a city known to you?

City centre offices

Liverpool has a very distinct yet compact office district lying to the north west of the shopping centre and extending one kilometre back from the River Mersey (Figure 3.6). Once again activities can be seen to cluster; this is especially the case with financial offices which are concentrated around the highest land value location at the junction of Chapel Street and Old Hall Street. Manufacturing offices are found along Old Hall Street and public administration in another cluster at the north-eastern end of the office area.

Much of what is known about office location has been developed in the large 'world cities' such as London and New York. The office districts of the City of London are shown on Figure 3.7 and it is obvious that functions have grouped. The force which pulls like functions and closely related functions, such as banking and finance, together

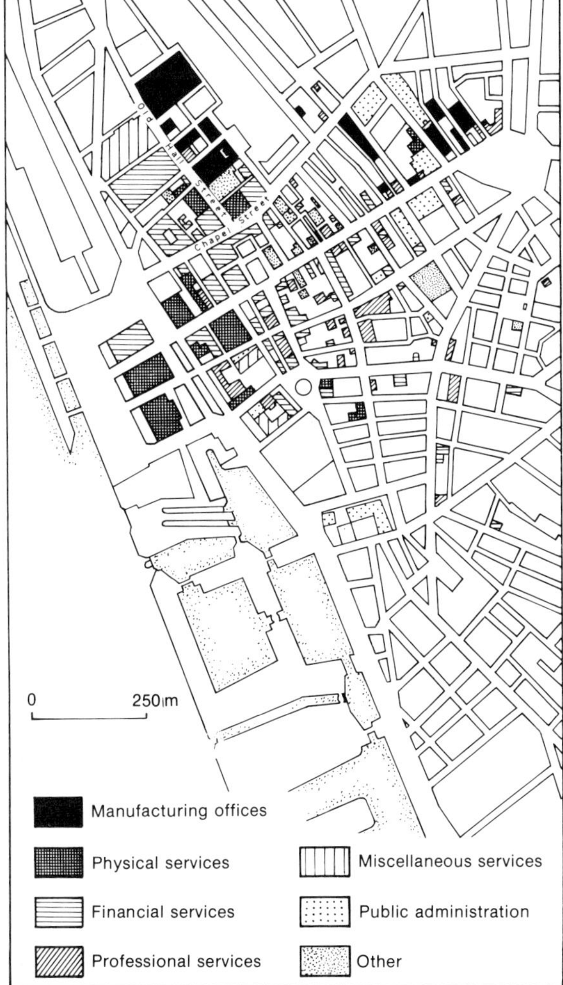

Figure 3.6 *The office district of Liverpool*

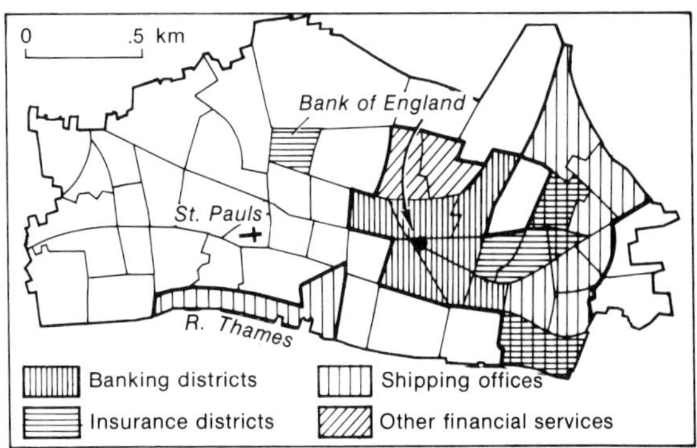

Figure 3.7 *The office districts of the City of London*

is termed **linkage** and locations for activities have been decided on the strength of the linkages to other activities.

Linkages take five major forms. First they can be **competitive** as in the case of rival shops or banks. Second they can be **complementary** because they interact in the way that an insurance company can use advertising agencies and graphic designers when placing advertisements in a newspaper. Third there are **ancilliary linkages** in that office workers need cafes, pubs and other lunchtime facilities. Fourthly there are **supply linkages** in that several companies may use the same printer or stationery supplier. Finally there are the complex **information linkages** which move between firms and are most aptly summed up at the trivial level by the line 'a rumour went round the City today . . .'. There are certain key points in the City such as the Bank of England, The Stock Exchange, Lloyds Insurance Building and the Commodity Trading Markets. One of the most unusual and unexpected is the cluster of fur traders around the Hudsons Bay Company Office in Great Trinity Lane, London which is also the home of most company headquarters.

The provincial cities are usually the home of branch offices or those offices providing goods and services to the local economy. Therefore employment in computing in Manchester, Leeds and Birmingham grew by 100% between 1976 and 1980, insurance by 77%, management consultants by 63%, finance by 56% and advertising by 29%. Much employment has been generated by branch offices of London companies. In Leeds, branch offices of London-based companies grew by 128% between 1976 and 1980. Manchester's branch offices grew more slowly (34%) probably because it is a more established provincial centre. Nevertheless, it is this growth in office employment allied to the growth in local and national government employment (at least until 1979) which has provided the impetus for the redevelopment of much of the city centre of Leeds.

Study activity

1 What proportion of your own city centre has been redeveloped? What type of activities now use the redeveloped properties? Try to find what was on these sites before redevelopment.

Redevelopment and land use conflicts

The physical presence of so many new office blocks in city centres is evidence enough of the vast growth in demand and the profits which can be made. Now that much of the core of many cities has been redeveloped interest has shifted to the frame, to the areas of mixed central area, industrial and residential uses on the inner edge of what Burgess termed the **zone in transition**. When the developer turns his attention to these areas conflicts often arise.

Coin Street is the name given to a large 5 hectare (12 acre) site close to London's Waterloo station on the South Bank of the Thames next to the National Theatre and facing the Embankment in the Law Courts area (Figure 3.8). It is an almost abandoned area of former warehouses, industry and a few flats. Because of its location close to a major railway terminus, it would make an ideal site for a large office and hotel complex on the edge of the central area of London. The land is owned mainly by the Greater London Council (GLC). Between 1977 and 1981 the GLC backed by a property developer, proceeded to move towards a scheme for approximately one million square feet of office space and about 200 houses. However, this scheme which was the brainchild of the Conservative-controlled GLC was vigorously opposed in two lengthy enquiries by the Borough of Lambeth which was Labour-controlled, and the Association of Waterloo Groups who wanted the area to provide mainly housing. One scheme suggested 360 houses. In 1981 the change in political control of the GLC to Labour resulted in all the office development proposals

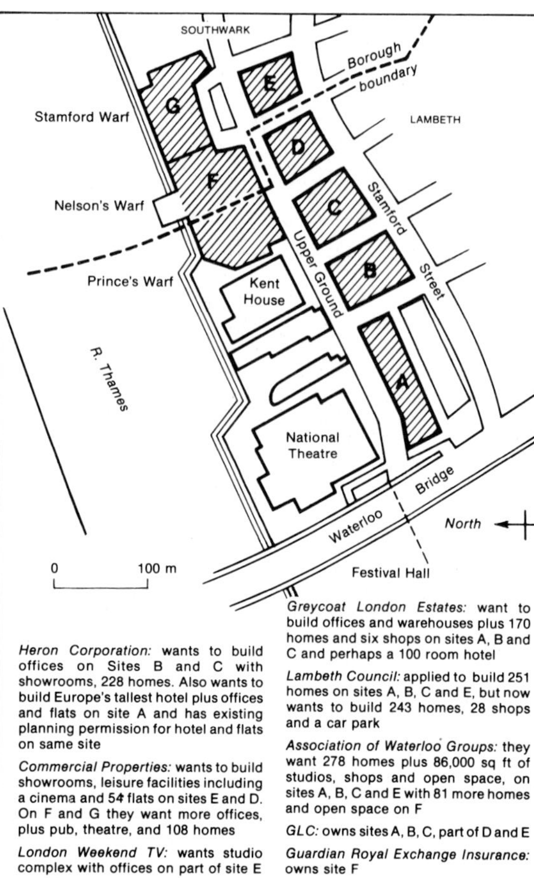

Figure 3.8 Coin Street site

being rejected and the future of the site was once again at the beginning of the long process of decision-making on its eventual use. The conflict is between two **interest groups**, the developers who see it as prime land for offices, and the local population who see it as a vital housing area close to the central area. The case also serves to illustrate the fact that land-uses do not arise solely from abstract theoretical forces but that political decisions by elected representatives who support particular causes and interests will also influence change in a city centre.

Study activity

Using the data on Figure 3.8, try to decide the best use for Coin Street.

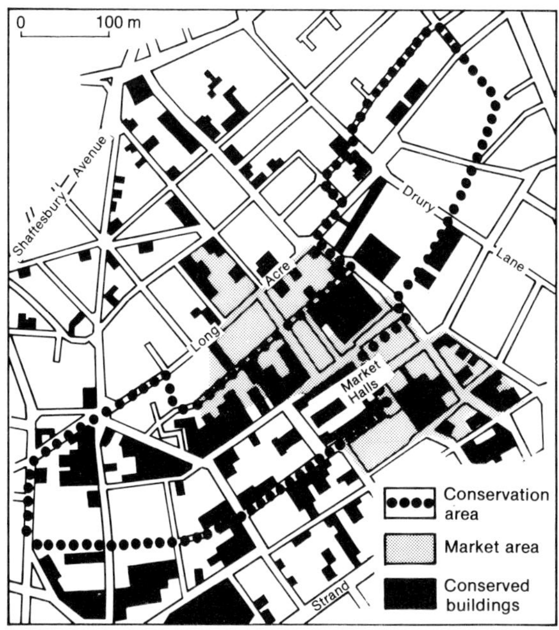

Figure 3.9 Covent Garden site

In other cases the conflict resulting from redevelopment has taken the form of the developer versus the conservation lobby. London's Covent Garden is a case in point (Figure 3.9). Here the abandonment of a site in the capital mid-way between the City and Westminster when the fruit and vegetable markets were moved to a modern site at Nine Elms was the key to another conflict of interests. Once again the development lobby partly aided by those who wanted improved roads was in favour of a **comprehensive redevelopment**, clearing the site and developing purpose-built offices. This scheme would have involved the destruction of the market halls and flats. In this case it was decided that the market halls should be maintained and they have been developed as a new, very trendy shopping and tourist area. The buildings around are acquiring a new lease of life as they are refurbished for more restaurants, galleries and boutiques. In this case the residents and the conservation lobby won, but as the area becomes more desirable will the original residents be able to afford the higher rents that will follow?

Les Halles in Paris is an identical site to Covent Garden (Figure 3.10). Here the 35 hectare site around the central Paris markets was abandoned in 1969 when the markets transferred to a 220 hectare site at Rungis in the south of the city. In this case there were strong pressures to build a modern office, shopping and hotel centre over one of the major Metro (underground) interchanges in Paris. The whole conflict lasted a decade and involved reconciling the interests of people who saw the destruction of the old market pavilions as the destruction of Paris' heritage with that of the developers in the form of the French government, the city of Paris and property developers. The result looks like some form of compromise. The market halls have gone, one to be rebuilt totally out of place in the suburbs, but the buildings in the surrounding area, dating from the seventeenth century have been improved and new social (council) apartments created. The main site has been redeveloped underground with a large shopping centre, car parks, swimming pool and postal facilities while the surface is to have a 5 hectare park, an hotel and some new offices and apartments. One part of the redevelopment area now contains the Pompidou Centre for the Arts and around this a similar upgrading of the ground

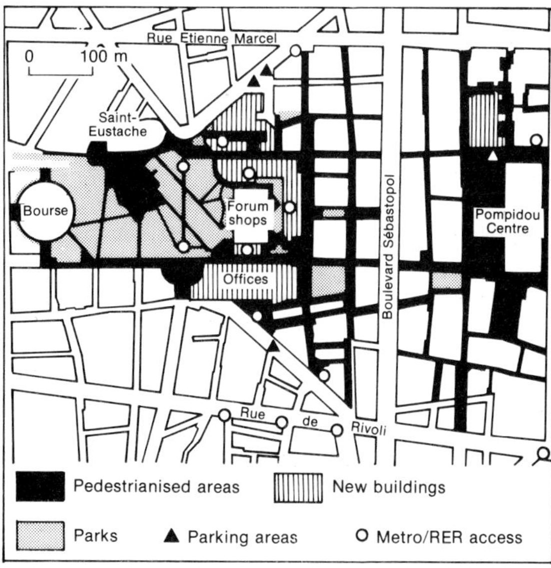

Figure 3.10 Les Halles

floor shops has occurred. The whole area will be a pedestrian precinct. This scheme which many feel has changed the character of the area represents a victory for the former French President Giscard d'Estaing and not one for the development lobby although their interests have been partly met. The loser would again seem to be the traditional local resident.

Study activity

1 At the end of the last section you were asked to consider redevelopment in a city. Have the types of conflict which we have described here been present in your city? If there is a case go and look at back numbers of the local paper either in the library or the paper's cuttings library and see if you can identify the contenders in the conflict and the outcome. Why do you think the result of the conflict was development, no change or limited change?

City centre recreation and tourism

All too frequently we consider the city centre solely as a place to work or shop and we ignore its other role which many see as a very important one for the future; that is providing for recreation and tourism. The city centre is a place that people visit as a part of their work and the housing of the visiting business man has been a traditional function for a long time. However, the working dinner or the evening 'on the town' sees the same individual making use of the recreational and tourist facilities of the city. **Tourism** is a long term activity involving visiting a place or area which normally entails residence away from home. Therefore a city centre can be one point on an itinerary for a day during a holiday or the location of a stay involving several days. Therefore Edinburgh or Bath might be a 24-hour stop in a tour whereas central Paris is the focus for a long weekend. **Recreation** is a much shorter term activity often involving just part of a day. It is home based. Activities such as visiting the medieval market and modern shopping have been viewed as recreation as much as the trip to visit the cathedral or museum, or a night out at a pub, restaurant or nightclub.

In central Newcastle there were five major hotels one of which was built next to the station. The station hotel quarter is very common in most cities. In central London the area south of King's Cross and Euston stations is full of small hotels. There is a similar location for hotels around the Gare St Lazare and Gare du Nord in Paris and around the main stations of Frankfurt and Munich. Birmingham has its Midland Hotel and a new hotel has been built at Southampton station. These hotels cater primarily for business visitors but, more recently, the larger hotels have broadened their appeal. Initially this involved the use of meeting rooms for business purposes during the day. The fate of many readers' 'A' levels and GCSEs will have been partly determined in these hotels which frequently house examiners' meetings! More recently the larger chains have moved into the 'weekend break' market to cater for the city centre tourist either as an individual, or as a part of a package tour. For these people the city centre location is an important part of the holiday with its access to the entertainment facilities of the city. Thus the Grainger Market, conserved Grey Street, the Quayside, the Keep, the Tyne Bridges and even the Metro can be a part of the tourist attraction offered by the Swallow Hotel in Newcastle. In London it will be the traditional sights which are within easy reach. Hotels are not the sole providers of tourist accommodation in the city centre. In Newcastle, the University rents out accommodation both to tourists and for larger scale conferences and, like most city centre educational institutions, is keen to use its residential accommodation outside the normal college terms.

The city centre tourist is a short stay visitor; in London he or she averages 3.3 days, and it is 3.5 and 2.2 days in Paris and Amsterdam respectively. Bath and Stratford-upon-Avon are, as we have seen, staging posts; international visitors tend to dominate the summer season whereas home based tourists are more likely to come out of season. Much of the city centre tourism is tied up with the conservation of historic monuments and townscapes. In Bath the tourist city focuses on the Abbey, Abbey Green and the Roman Baths and extends through the centre to Pulteney Bridge and the Octagon (Figure 3.11). The three remaining foci are beyond the centre although The Circus and the Assembly Rooms are part of the frame because the streets include many professional offices. The tourist visit to Bath is an excursion on foot and the routes between the attractions are the prime locations for the souvenir shops, cafes and wine bars. However, the demands of visitors in large numbers do conflict with the needs of conservation. Car and bus parks are needed and do intrude, causing controversy as in the case of the Walcot Street site in Bath. One wonders whether hoards of visitors moving in organised groups around the Baths really do appreciate the serenity or technical achievements of the Roman Baths.

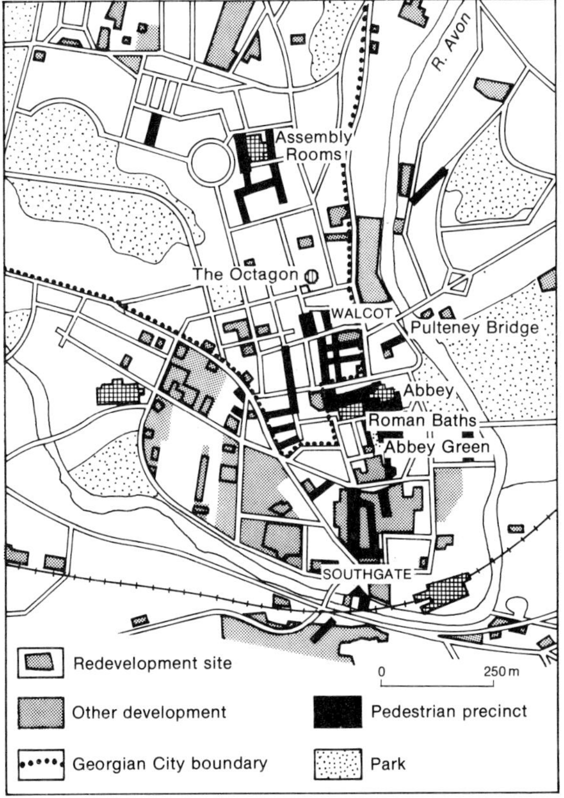

Figure 3.11 Bath – a tourist city

Obviously the tourist function does overlap with the recreation function, particularly at weekends. The overlap is greatest where there is a distinct museum quarter as in London's South Kensington, and the Rijksmuseum complex in Amsterdam although the same overlapping functions can be seen in the Parisian museums which are among the top tourist attractions of the city (Figure 3.12).

Museums are just one aspect of the growing city centre leisure industry. While the cinema is declining from its already minor importance in city centres, most British cities do still have a struggling theatre and concert hall and only in London can one find a distinct theatre and cinema district. Nightlife districts where activities such as bars, restaurants and nightclubs cluster are more developed in Western Europe than in all but the larger British cities. The vice, prostitution night life reputation of Soho is well known and similar areas exist in most large cities such as Rue St Denis and Pigalle in Paris, Zeedijk in Amsterdam and the Reeperbahn in Hamburg. These are the parts of a centre which may appear semi-derelict at 10.00 a.m. but by midnight are crowded with visitors.

Study question

1 What are the problems caused by the growth of a central leisure area in a city? Who gains and who loses?

Study activity

1 Make an inventory of the tourist and recreation facilities in the centre of your home town. Categorise them according to who they appeal to and estimate the number of visitors. How could these facilities be improved to the benefit of the town?

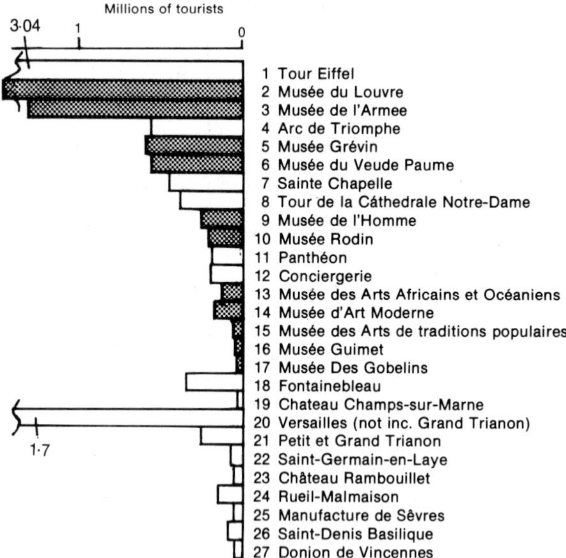

Figure 3.12 Tourist attractions in Paris

The city centre in Eastern Europe

As we saw in Chapter 2 there is no land market within the socialist countries and therefore the development value of land and buildings is considerably reduced as a result. In addition with state banking and finance and, to a certain extent, state-run retailing there is less demand for growth and change in the city centre which has a very distinctive character. Without the commercial pressures for development it has been much more easy to accommodate people within the central area and it has been relatively easy although somewhat costly to conserve the historic core. In the case of Warsaw this did involve the rebuilding stone by stone of Stare Miasto after the destruction of the Second World War. Similarly, the city core of Leningrad has been carefully conserved due to the city's historic role as a former capital of Russia. Many city centres have been conserved in part and in part extended, typically those cities that suffered heavy war damage such as Warsaw and Hauptstadt-Berlin (East Berlin).

In the rebuilding of Hauptstadt-Berlin (Figure 3.13) the city centre was to reflect the prestige of the state and the new social order of socialism. Therefore cultural and educational facilities were important as were the state ministeries and the workers' organisations. The Unter den Linden area also includes embassies, notably that of the USSR, and other major state organisations such as the Academy of Sciences. It has a much lower density of buildings because of the lack of competing functions. There are now only three insurance offices controlling the whole German Democratic Republic and a single legal collective. The number of retail outlets is only 75, there are only four airline ticket offices and only one photographic outlet for Karl Zeiss, Jena. The other emphasis has been to create major processional streets such as Unter den Linden and Karl Marx Allee and squares for state organised public assemblies such as Marx Engels Platz (Figure 3.13). While Berlin-Hauptstadt is not typical in that it is only half of a divided Berlin it does illustrate the principles of city centre development where rebuilding was possible.

Elsewhere in Eastern Europe new city centres are being grafted on to the old towns. Again the high density of buildings in a centre such as Old Katowice, in Poland, contrast with the open, parkland layout of the new centre flanking the appropriately named, processional, Red Army Square. The new area contains a large number of cultural and sporting facilities besides a few major offices and shops. A similar new centre has been built in Zagreb, Yugoslavia.

In the USSR there is a similar paucity of retail outlets in the centre of Moscow or Leningrad and even major stores such as GUM are hangovers from pre-1918. Shops are in the suburbs and much of the administration other than the Kremlin is spread through the city. The centre has a strong cultural and symbolic role epitomised by Red Square and Lenin's mausoleum. More recently the open plan of the city centres has been criticised and attempts have been made to try and give land some theoretical value so that the most central area of a city can be used more effeciently. The outcome has been an attempt to build clusters of activities in new highrise blocks which are beginning to appear in Moscow.

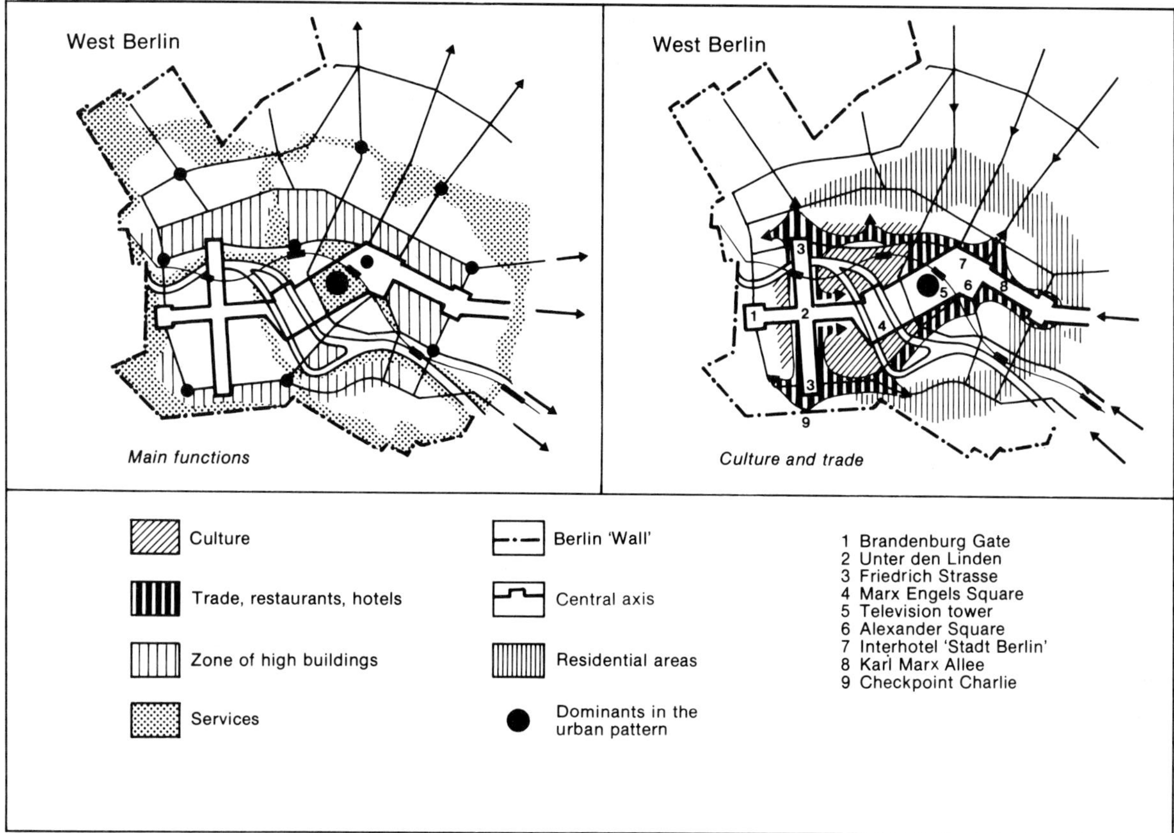

Figure 3.13 A socialist city centre – Hauptstadt-Berlin

City centres in the future

So far in this chapter we have looked at the nature of the central area of British cities and have noted some of the variations in other cultures. The centre is the dynamo which keeps the rest of a city going and only in a few exceptional cases such as the cities of sun belt USA, is there no real centre as we would expect. But what will the city centre look like in the future? This is an open discussion and in no way can it be regarded as definitive because the further into the future we look the greater are the imponderables. Nevertheless, the possibilities are sketched here so that you can discuss the alternatives.

One of the themes which have been outlined so far is the city centre as a place of employment. Developments in electronic technology will possibly alter employment prospects very radically. The 'micro-chip revolution' or the introduction of new computer-based technologies is expected to reduce employment. Word processors, computer-controlled typewriters that can undertake many secretarial duties of a routine kind could remove nine out of every ten secretaries from employment. Information could be filed on tapes and updated or corrected when necessary so removing the need for retyping. It is possible that the word processor and other computer terminal facilities could be installed at home so that there would be no need to journey to work other than from the breakfast table to the terminals! In the field of retailing new methods of goods handling and scanners which automatically record sales by product will reduce the numbers involved in ordering and accounts. Automation in the field of banking including experiments which would enable bank cash cards to be used in the supermarket checkout to automatically transfer funds from the personal account to the shop's account would also produce labour savings. The jobs which would remain would be either very skilled management or totally unskilled tasks. Employment would be both reduced and **deskilled**, ie. few skilled jobs would be needed. What would be the effect on the use of the present city centre buildings of such a trend?

A second future which emerges from the discussion earlier in the chapter is that of the city centre as a place for enjoyment. We are increasingly concerned by the quality of life in the city centre. Does this just mean the maintenance of cultural facilities or does it entail more than putting parts of the centre into quarantine? How do we use the past, provide access to it for all without destroying the past by the sheer volume of visitors?

If we are to make the city a place to visit how do we go about adapting the space behind the street frontage for new uses? Should more people be encouraged to live in the centre? If so how do we encourage owners to adapt the area above shops rather than leave it empty because residences over shops are a security risk? The centre as a place of pleasure and environmental quality may be a worthy ideal but how do we achieve it?

This brings us to a third consideration for the future of the city centre. Very frequently in discussing change we have noted those who gain and those who loose. New offices and new shops benefit the owners and provide jobs, as does entertainment and hotels. Very frequently improving an area removes the long term residents because they cannot afford the rents. They are replaced by the more affluent groups who will often live in the same refurbished building, a process known as **gentrification** which occurs both in the centre and the inner suburbs. The centre of big cities are fast becoming gentrified. Paris of the rich is replacing Paris of the people as new apartment blocks and refurbished older apartment blocks attract the middle classes to live close to the attractions which they value. The same has occurred in Mayfair and, as in parts of west central Paris, the new occupiers are the affluent foreign population working for international companies or representing the oil-rich countries. The old buildings have been improved but as we saw in the Covent Garden case, for whom?

This leads us to a fourth debating point. Who benefits from the conservation of parts of the city centre? Conservation can leave areas with ground floor uses but without a use for the upper storeys. This is the case in parts of Grey Street, Newcastle, which is considered the finest curved Regency street in Western Europe, and in nearby Pilgrim Street. Glance upwards in the conserved core of many towns and it is soon apparent that the upper storeys are underused. Should conservation also include increasing the utility of the space behind the picturesque facade? Are professional offices the best use for some of our conserved centres? Long Lane in Leicester is an example of conservation bringing a host of solicitors, architects and accountants into elegant regency dwellings. Is it possible to devise ways in which an adequate return on investment could be ensured by keeping properties as residences? If so, could this policy ensure that some space is devoted to the lower income earners and if not, why not?

The final problem for the future of the city centre is that of transport. It takes on two dimensions, that of movement in the city centre and that of movement to and from centres. Within the centre the need to segregate pedestrian and vehicle traffic has been a consistent planning objective for over 20 years and most cities now boast pedestrianised shopping streets as we noted earlier. Pedestrian precincts are most suited for the car users but what kind of access problems do they pose for the elderly, the disabled and those dependent on public transport? They also pose delivery problems especially in cities where conservation schemes prevent the development of new access routes. Pedestrian schemes frequently go hand in hand with the creation of inner

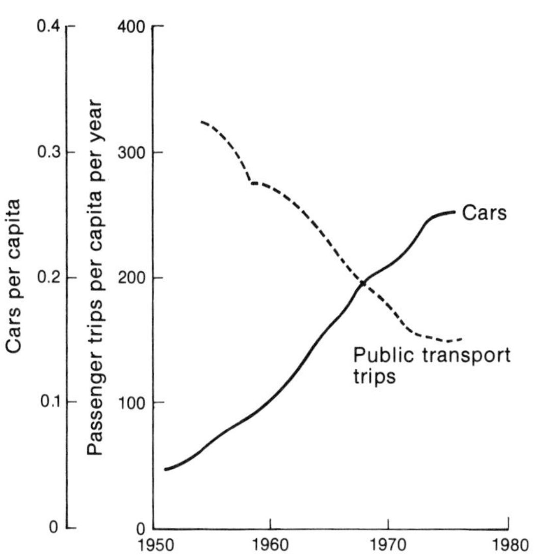

Figure 3.14 *Trends in car ownership and public transport*

ring routes such as the Newcastle urban motorway or the ring around Coventry which tend to cut the centre off from the surrounding areas.

Study activity

Look at a city centre and try to establish what the effects of either increasing the pedestrian area or building an extension to a partly completed inner ring route would be. What would be the costs and what would be the benefits of your ideas; in other words who wins and who loses?

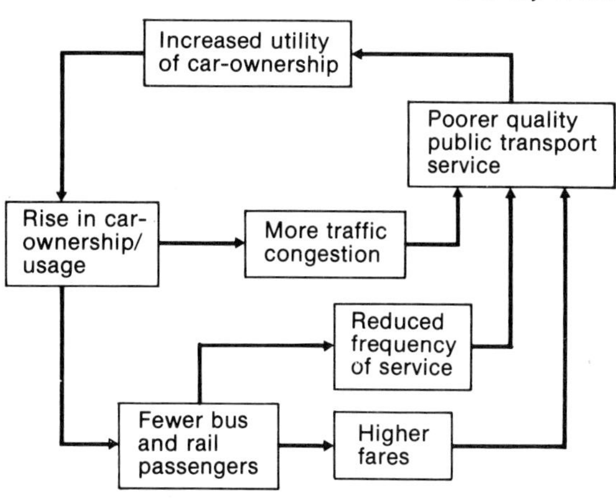

Figure 3.15 *Cumulative decline of public transport*

Increased car ownership has produced a decline in the number of trips by public transport (Figure 3.14). The effect on public transport is that fares go up and services are further reduced. This can be seen as a cumulative process (Figure 3.15) which disadvantages the old, the young, the young mother with children at home and the poorer non-car owners and, at the same time, alters the nature of the city centre. If the city centre is costly and difficult to reach will it remain the focus of urban life in the future? Should public transport to the city centre be made more attractive and if so, what measures are needed to do this? Some cities have embarked on schemes to maintain and improve public transport access. The Tyne and Wear Metro is one such case which has linked people in the region to the centre at a cost of £160.4 million (Figure 3.16).

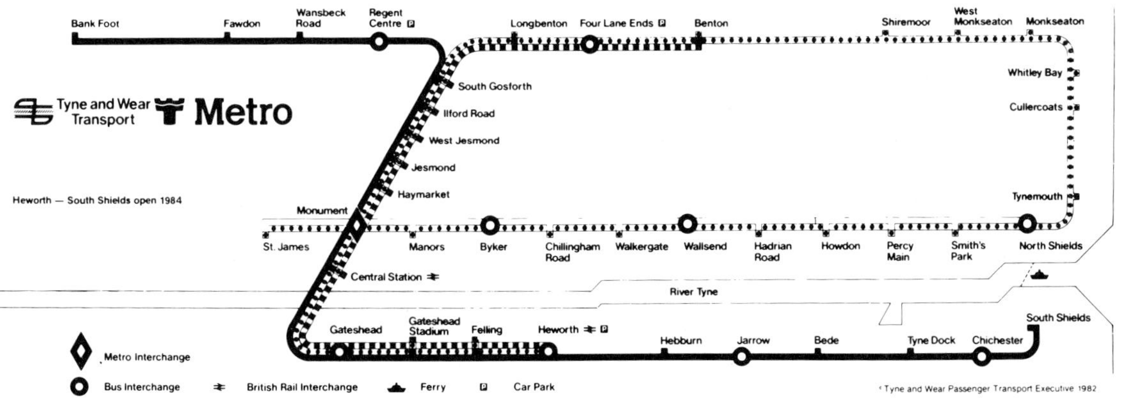

Figure 3.16 *Tyne and Wear Metro*

4

Suburban growth

By far the largest part of the modern city's area is its suburbs. In this chapter we are going to examine the development, nature and problems of the suburbs. Suburbs are not all 'little boxes made of ticky tacky', the homes of the aspiring middle classes in the words of the folk singer Pete Seager. They are a mixture of functions; predominantly residential but with large areas devoted to industry, open space and transport together with smaller more concentrated areas of retailing, offices and recreation.

The spread of the suburbs in Britain since 1920 can be seen as a series of waves each carrying new activities away from the city centre to the suburbs.

Study activity

1 Approximately what proportion of the area of your home town has been developed since 1920? What building forms and street layouts are typical of these developments? Can you identify the same street layouts on an OS map of a town which you do not know?
2 What factors have influenced the growth of a town? If you have forgotten read Chapter 2 again!

The first wave: people

The prime factor in the spread of suburbs has been the movement of people out from the city. In Chapter 2 we noted several factors such as the role of transport and developers. However for growth to occur there must have been some pressure of population. The pressure came both from the natural increase of population in cities and from migration to the cities which in turn increased the demand for homes. The developers then helped to fulfil this demand aided and abetted by improvements in transport provision to and from the city. Increasing affluence also enabled the aspiring to obtain a mortgage of maybe £750 for a semi-detached three bedroom house in Buckhurst Hill (London) in 1937. At the same time the vacated terrace house in Leyton which had been rented could be relet to a Welsh family who had originally moved into rooms in Stepney. In this way affluence and the growth of population enabled property to **filter** or move down through the social groups. Likewise the large Victorian villa might become split into two houses and finally subdivided for immigrants during the 1950s. Demand was also fuelled by Britain's suburban tradition which has left many old rural settlements engulfed by bungalows yet still called 'the village'.

A major contributor to the spread of suburbs in British cities has been the local authority which has been responsible for the building of large estates of **council houses** which are frequently called **public housing** or **social housing** because they have been subsidised in one form or another by central and local government. The impact of the estates on the spread of the town is most striking. Local authorities after 1945 were attempting to fulfil the demand for housing. Since then, initially on their own, and, after 1954, with the rebirth of private housing construction, the authorities have built 49% of the housing in England and Wales. Cinema newsreels of the 1950s and 1960s proclaimed Kirby (Liverpool), Leigh Park (Portsmouth) and Debden (LCC) as the ideal housing programme for the new Britain. This post war centrifugal movement of people can be clearly seen in the map of population change from 1951 to 1961 for the London area (Figure 4.1).

The first wave of suburban growth caused by people has continued to spread outwards to the rural areas, often up to thirty miles around larger cities, so that the village is rarely an agricultural settlement. Villages and old market towns today are **commuter settlements** more likely to be populated by industrial and office managers than farm workers. They are an integral part of the phenomenon of counterurbanisation which we examined in Chapter 1.

Study activity

1 Choose a village near to a town and estimate from your knowledge the proportion of the homes occupied by commuters. What types of house are occupied by commuters? How could you obtain a more accurate picture of the amount and destination of commuting from the village?

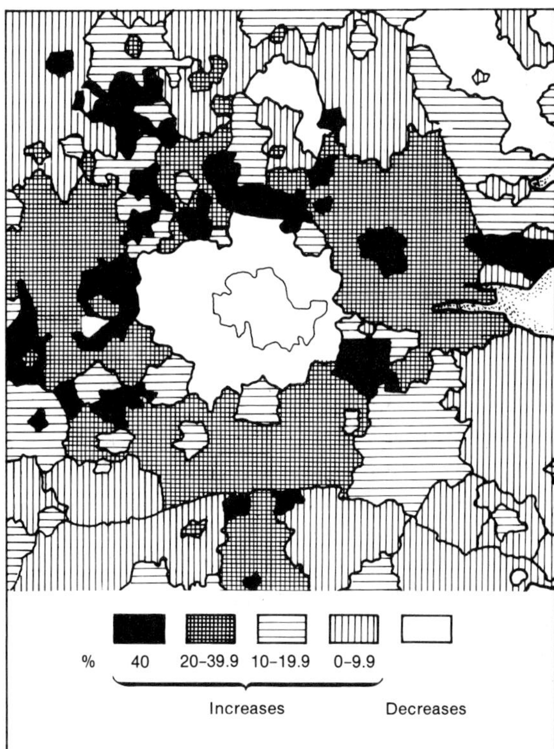

Figure 4.1 1951–61 Population change in London

The second wave: employment

The movement of jobs to the suburbs soon followed that of population. This was particularly the case in the inter-war period when new suburban industrial zones began to be developed to supply the consumer products that were fast becoming fashionable. In London the Park Royal area of the Great West Road was developed between the wars and the old exhibition halls of the Wembley Empire Exhibition of 1927 were converted to provide more industrial space. In other areas the government's efforts to create the conditions for new jobs saw the development of **trading estates** such as Treforest just outside Cardiff and the Team Valley estate on the fringe of Gateshead.

The pattern of industrial development outside the major inner city, railside and port industrial areas had been set by the Second World War. After the War more industrial estates were developed closer to the labour market, in the suburbs of almost every city. The foci for the new industrial areas were the major roads leading into the city such as the Millbrook area of Southampton; alongside ring roads such as the southern ring around Nürnberg; major areas of flat land ideal for assembly line industries such as the Speke area of Merseyside; and around major airports such as Heathrow. In the **new towns** and **expanded towns** (see chapter 6) of the 1950s and 1960s industrial areas were invariably large areas on the outskirts of the town such as the northern side of Crawley and Houndsmills in Basingstoke.

It is possible to analyse the type of industry that is found in these areas and, at the same time, explain why industry has appeared to abandon its traditional urban locations. A useful framework for studying industrial areas of a city is to find out whether the firms which are present are or were new when they established themselves in a location. These firms can be called **births**. Other firms might have moved from other areas and can be called **transfers**. Transfers can be of two types the first of which involves the closing of the previous premises and the second the expansion into a new factory which is a branch of one in the main city. Branch plants can also be births if their parent company is in another city. Finally there are those firms which collapse or are taken over which we can call **deaths** or **closure rates**.

A study of Glasgow attempted to look at the births, deaths and transfers of firms to see how much of the industrial change in a city is based on each of the three factors. In the period 1958 to 1968 the number of factories in Glasgow declined by 6% with the heaviest decline in the centre. The death rate in the surrounding towns and the suburbs was even higher than the inner city but the real problem was the very low birth rate of firms in the inner city. In addition the new factories in the Glasgow inner area were employing half as many people on average than the outer city factories. New premises, with good road access to markets and low rents were a definite attraction.

A similar study of industry in London between 1966 and 1974 has shown that the decline of industry in the older areas is caused as much by the death and shrinkage of old workshops (67% of the loss of 390000 industrial job losses) as by movement out of the more dynamic, modern, consumer oriented factories (27% of industrial jobs). Those that moved wanted more space, preferably on one floor in a more modern building. The land costs were lower as were rents. The moves were generally to the outer suburbs and the new towns with only the larger firms being attracted out of the London region to the development regions. In the case of London the outer suburbs lost jobs to other regions of Britain as well. The new firms did not come to the vacated premises; instead they preferred the new estates of the suburbs or beyond. In this way the notion that the older industrial areas of cities were **seed bed** or **nursery** for new companies has been seriously called into question.

Study activity

1 Using a local trading estate or industrial area attempt to find out how many firms grew up there and how many transferred from elsewhere. Which firms have expanded since arrival and which, if any, have died?

2 Suggest the potential location for a new industrial area in your town and explain why you think it would be suitable. This is best done with the aid of 1:50000 or 1:25000 Ordnance Survey maps to help your deliberations.

The third wave: retailing

Shopping provision has also spread from the city centre although, as we saw in Chapter 3, the central areas of European cities have been forced to adapt to counter competition from the new suburban shops. In the period 1919 to 1939 the new housing areas frequently contained new **shopping parades**, often on the main roads but set back with their own service road in front. This pattern of providing shops in **ribbons** or 20 or so units continued after the 1939–45 war. Figure 4.2 shows one such ribbon in suburban Portsmouth. Today these small centres cater for local needs and sell **low order goods**, eg.

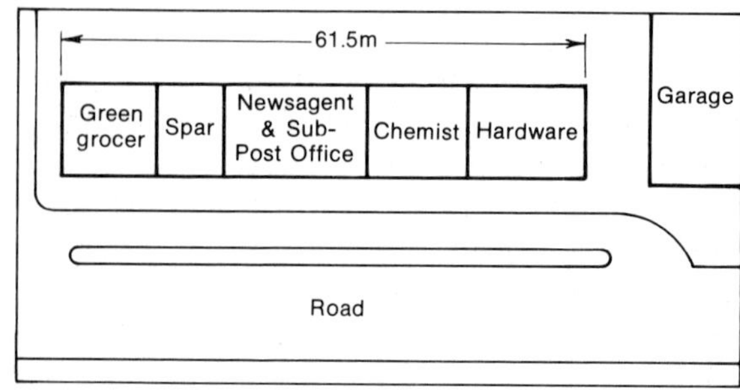

Figure 4.2 Suburban shopping ribbon at Widley

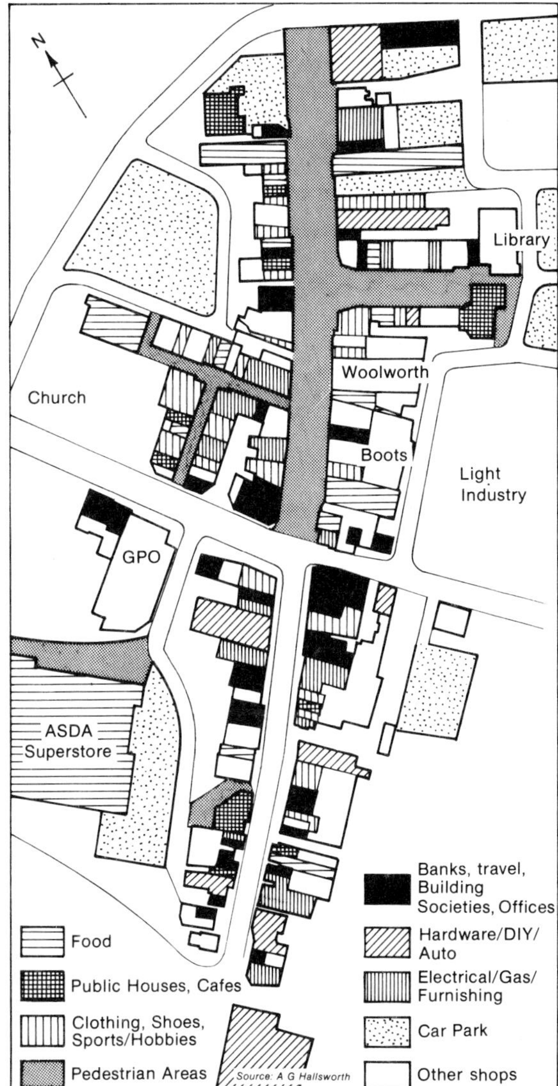

Figure 4.3 *Waterlooville, Portsmouth*

convenience goods and food, rather than **consumer** goods, eg. electrical equipment.

The post war period has also seen the growth and development of existing small nuclei in the outer suburbs of towns and the building of new centres to cater for some of the large scale suburban housing developments. The latter are frequently associated with council estates and are part of the planned provision of shopping for these areas.

The expansion of pre-existing small centres has also been a common form of retail development in the suburbs. Waterlooville (Figure 4.3) is a typical case of this type of development outside Portsmouth. The ribbon of shops along the A3 focusing on the crossroads has been modernised by providing new frontages to older buildings and by demolishing old buildings and replacing them with shops with offices above. Two small pedestrian precincts were built in the 1960s leading to car parks and with a supermarket and the library as foci. More recently a large superstore with its own car park has been constructed by ASDA to the south west of the centre so increasing the attractiveness of the centre. This store covers 6000 sq metres and sells both food and a wide range of non-food items on six days a week with opening hours stretched on four nights to either 20.00 or 21.00 hours.

Study activity

1 Prepare a map of the functions of a suburban shopping centre near to you.
2 Can you note any changes which have taken place in the last 10 years? Why have these changes occurred?
3 It might be possible to analyse the distribution of shops in the same way as on p 37.

Most recently the suburbs have seen the growth of other forms of retailing. Havant Hypermarket opened in 1980 between Leigh Park and Waterlooville (Figure 2.1). Britain's first **hypermarket**, a large purpose built retail outlet with car parks, operated by one company and selling both food and non-food items, was opened at Caerphilly in 1972. The same company has a hypermarket at Chandler's Ford outside Southampton (Figure 4.4a). These developments are more dependent on the car-borne shopper (Havant is on the A3M although buses do stop in the car park area). Their opening hours, which enable family evening shopping, and cheap petrol attract the mobile shopper keen on **one stop shopping**. Very

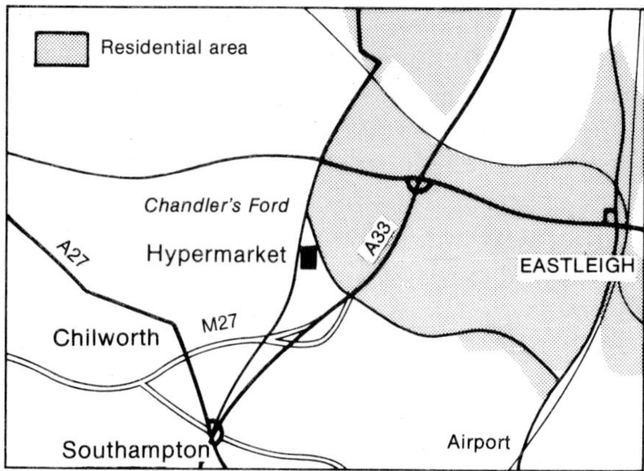

Figure 4.4a Hypermarket location at Chandler's Ford

frequently the location of hypermarkets is with a certain **time distance** (normally 20–40 minutes) of a large population who have high or above average spending power. They are a much more familiar sight in France where cities such as Orleans have one on each side of town (Figure 4.4b).

The other new type of centre is the isolated purpose-built, covered, air-conditioned shopping centre with large car parks of which the sole British example is Brent Cross in north west London which was opened in 1976 (Figure 4.5). There are at least six such developments around Paris of which the earliest, most sophisticated, but by no means largest example, is Parly II near Versailles (Figure 4.6). This type of development has been most popular in the USA and Canada of which the Eastridge Mall at San José, Woodfield Mall at Schaumberg, Chicago (the largest) and Yorkdale, Toronto are three examples. The plan in Figure 4.7 is of the Place Laurier scheme in the western suburb of St Foy, Quebec City. This particular scheme, like that at Woodfield, is a three storeyed assembly of shops with two office towers above (unlike most North American examples). It is more complex than the British and French examples which are generally of a dumbbell shape with **anchor stores** at either end to attract and provide the flow of pedestrians through the centre. The stores are generally high quality. These new groupings of several hundred shops, frequently on the richer side of town and well served by modern motorways and freeways have brought about a major shift in the location of people's shopping. With 18 such centres around Chicago it is no wonder that central area retailing has stagnated. A similar conse-

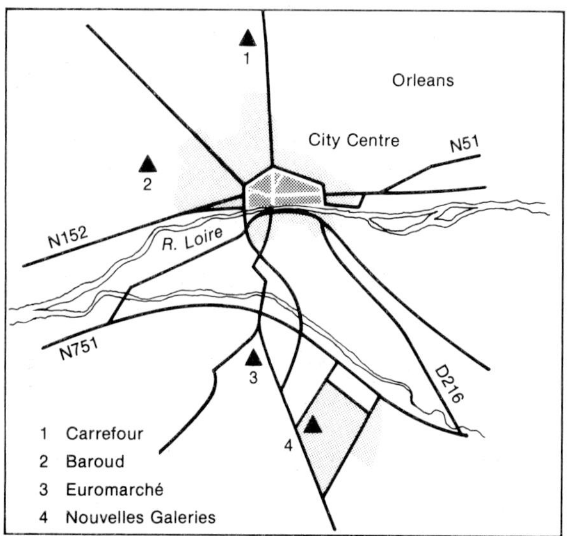

Figure 4.4b Hypermarket location at Orleans

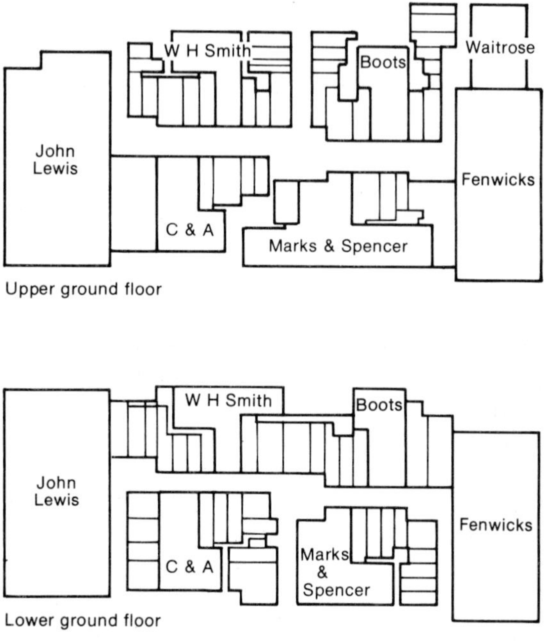

Figure 4.5 Brent Cross

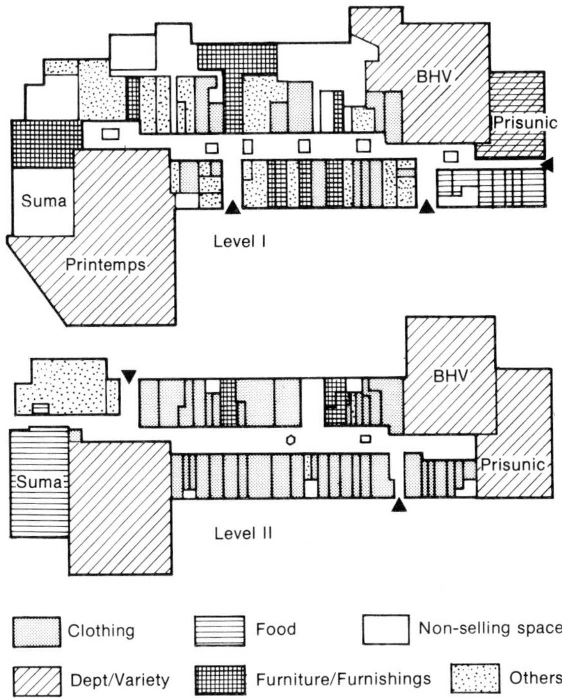

Figure 4.6 *Parly II, Versailles*

quence has been predicted for European cities where these centres have been developed although rarely does the number in an area approach that of Paris or Chicago. For instance only two have been developed in the Ruhr, one of which was so early that it has remained uncovered like the traditional shopping centre. Many are being developed to form the focus of new suburban housing developments such as Süd Centrum in Nürnberg's Langwasser and Chorweiler, Cologne.

With the outward spread of industry and retailing the need for wholesaling and warehousing to remain in or near the city centre has also decreased. Warehousing and wholesaling of general merchandise has declined in the centre of cities as the older buildings have been demolished and as the new retail groups develop their own supplies which do away with the need for the middle men. In the case of food wholesaling the location of major food markets has also been the subject of decentralisation. Covent Garden market has moved across the Thames. More recently London's Billingsgate market has been closed and moved eastwards to the Isle of Dogs. Rungis (Chapter 3) is on a 220 hectare site next to Orly airport and on the motorway and rail routes from the south. It employs 17000 people. The move of the Chicago stockyards by 40 miles to Joliet is another case. Decentralisation in both of these cases has been problematic because new forms of retailing, such as the supermarket chains, have developed their own warehousing points. Some supermarkets, by buying direct, eliminate all middle organisation, as ASDA do in Britain,

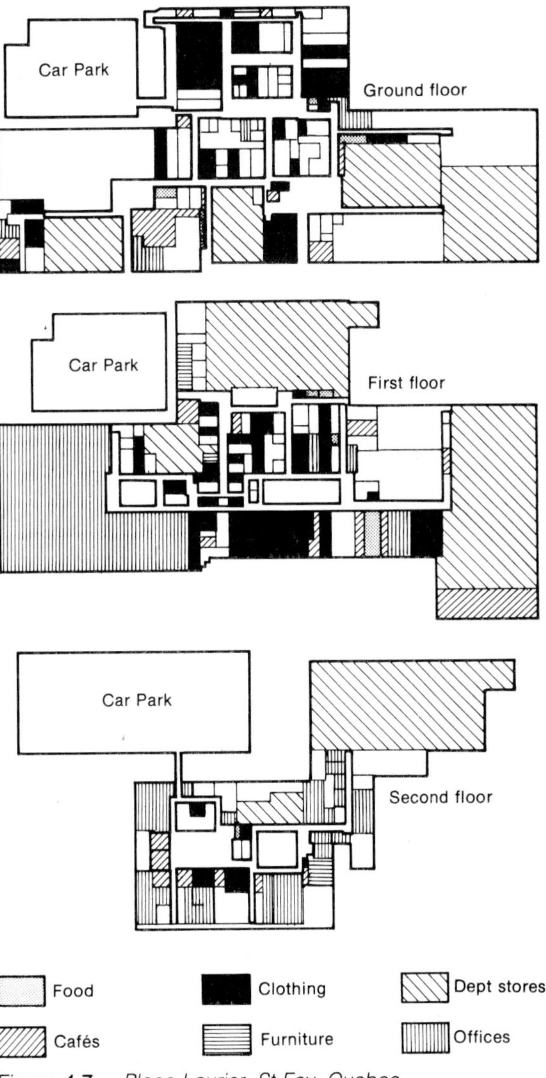

Figure 4.7 *Place Laurier, St Foy, Quebec*

Study activity

1 Try to make a list of the good and bad points of out-of-town retailing developments.
2 Is there a location near your home town where an out-of-town centre could be developed? Use a 1:50000 or 1:25000 map to help in the choice of sites. Justify your choice of site.

and have reduced the profitability of the new wholesale markets.

The fourth wave: offices

Office employment has also developed more strongly outside major cities in recent years and is therefore the fourth wave of activities to move to the suburbs. In recent years there has been a considerable demand for office space in the major world cities such as London, Paris, Frankfurt and New York. This demand has been fuelled by the growth in the size of industrial companies both as a result of expansion and as a result of mergers which have created the need for larger headquarters. At the same time banking, finance, investment and trade have also grown. Government also grew with more civil servants needed to administer each new law or change of law. In this way the office economy of the capital cities grew, putting pressure on space, and forcing up rents because of the demand. Increased congestion resulted as more people commuted to work in the City of London and Westminster.

In the London area the Croydon council took steps to encourage offices to relocate to the town centre and over a period of 25 years 30000 new office jobs were moved to Croydon. The effect on the town centre can be seen in Figure 4.8. Other offices were built either at nodes in the London suburbs such as Sutton and Kingston or at railway stations such as New Malden. Other offices have moved westwards to the area around Heathrow Airport. In all cases the relocating firms were seeking new premises with lower rents and staff costs and moving into the areas which supplied the office with labour. The government attempted to steer both civil service and private offices away from London and the south east in the period 1964–1979 through the activities of the Location of Offices Bureau. The effect was to provide major office growth in, for example, Durham (Post Office Savings), Harlow (BP) and Ipswich (GRE Insurance) which was normally in or close by the town centres. The type of activity which was best able to move to these locations was the routine work or paper processing such as the issuing of insurance renewals which did not need expensive space in a London office. On the other hand most companies who decentralised office functions left their main, decision-making office in London close to the sources of finance in the City preferring to decentralise the everyday work.

In some cases decentralised offices have become major employment centres in the suburbs of the new city locations. IBM (UK) are developing a major office node for 2500 employees on reclaimed land in Portsmouth Harbour (Figure 2.1). In Newcastle the DHSS office complex at Long Benton, which has the dubious honour of being the largest single office complex in Britain, is another example although this is not strictly the product of a move from London.

Outside London most city authorities have striven to provide office jobs away from the centre. The Regency centre in the northern suburbs of Newcastle has been built at a new metro station. Other cities have permitted office developments in and around growing or new suburban shopping centres and

Study question

Outline the possible disadvantages of city centre food wholesaling as at Covent Garden. Who would have been interested in the removal of Covent Garden to Nine Elms and why?

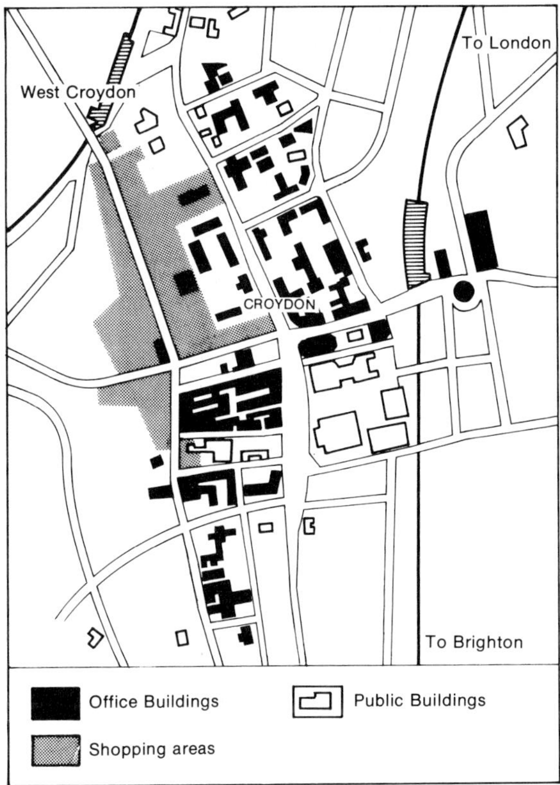

Figure 4.8 Croydon's offices

airports. Thus the plans for the Rungis area also included a shopping centre, Belle Epine, and offices. The Place Laurier scheme as we saw had two office towers. Elsewhere offices are merely the premises over shops and often converted houses, particularly the more imposing Georgian and Victorian houses which appeal to the professions as locations for offices.

Although not strictly office work it seems appropriate to include the suburban growth of the **quaternary** sector of employment (research and development) here. The new universities are frequently in the outer suburbs for instance Sussex University at Falmer outside Brighton and Bath University on Claverton Down. Research establishments have also developed in the rural fringes of towns. Country houses have become favoured locations for company training schools and research sections. IBM research laboratories at Hursley near Winchester and in the hills outside San José, California, are two examples while the science park outside Nice is a deliberate attempt by the French government to create a suburban research centre in a highly desirable area of France.

Study activity

1 Where are the major clusters of offices in your city? Are there any differences between the offices in the city centre and suburbs in terms of type of work, numbers employed and type of building?

Other suburban developments

In the wake of industrial, office and warehousing developments in the suburbs there has been a set of allied developments to service the new areas. Visiting businessmen arrive in cities more frequently by air or road transport than by railway. It is therefore hardly surprising that the city centre hotel districts, which are frequently close to the main railway stations, have been challenged by new hotels springing up at key locations in the suburbs. Very frequently the largest cities hotels are found close by or along the main route to the airport so servicing the needs of both aircrew and passengers. These hotels frequently provide conference facilities for businesses especially those businesses with large international functions who can fly executives in for a day's conference.

New hotels in intermediate locations between the airport and the city centre are becoming increasingly common. Examples of these are the Holiday Inn at Wideopen, Tyneside and the Post House, Edinburgh. Alternatively the location can be just off the main motorway exit for a town, such as the Post House at Reading. The Holiday Inn, Portsmouth (Figure 2.1) combines a location adjacent to IBM's UK headquarters with easy access by 5km of motorway to the channel ferry terminal. In fact, office parks are becoming a very important locational pull for major hotels in West Germany. The rapidly developing Arabella Park in eastern Munich contains two large hotels and the completed north Dusseldorf Park and Frankfurt Niederrad both contain large hotels catering primarily for the business executive market.

Nevertheless these hotels can and do cater for urban tourism by arrangements for cheaper weekend stays and their location is convenient in terms of access for short term tourist visits. Smaller hotels and guest houses on the major access routes into towns have also increased. The main road from the south into Edinburgh has several, as do the routes into most of the seaside resorts. A locational typology for hotels can be seen in Figure 4.9.

Conclusion

The evolution of the form of cities has resulted in the substantial growth of major foci of economic and service activity within the suburbs. This merits our attention because of the common factors that have aided the growth of industrial estates, office parks, shopping centres, hotels and conference centres. Accessibility, labour supply, modern appropriate buildings and changes in technology are common to all our case studies.

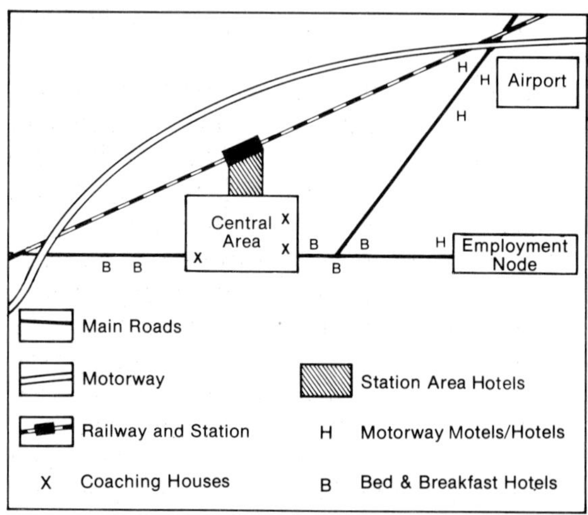

Figure 4.9 A locational typology for hotels in a European city

Study activity

1 Take any major route entering your home town or city and map the functions that have located along its outer section. To what extent are these functions taking advantage of accessibility and other adjacent functions?
2 A major hotel chain is anxious to open a 250 room hotel with conference and recreational facilities, such as a swimming pool, sauna and restaurants, in your nearest city. Using a 1:25000 map to help you identify potential sites, attempt to outline the advantages and disadvantages of the sites.

However, the most important factor of all is probably the inexorable drift of people to the suburbs, the counter-urbanisation pressure we noted in Chapter 1.

Revision

1 Define the following: filtering, trading estates, the birth and death of firms, hypermarket, quasi-retail sector, superstore.
2 Can you remember the sequence of movement to the suburbs?
3 What factors have influenced the decentralisation of economic activities in cities?
4 Who gains from decentralising economic activities and who loses?

5

Urban social geography

By far the largest user of space in the city is housing, which is also one of the most dynamic elements in the city. People move house, new houses are built, houses decline in quality. We have already seen in Chapters 2 and 4 how the general age of housing is younger at greater distances from the city centre, with the exception of the areas of renewal. We have also noted that certain types of residential area appear to be located in sectors. In this section we can now attempt to identify more rigorously the variety of areas which comprise this largest part of a city's space.

Study activity

Attempt to categorise the different types of housing areas in your home town. Draw a quick sketch of them. On what basis did you divide the areas?

If you attempted the activity suggested above, or even asked a friend to do it, it is probable that the divisions which you made were based on one or more of the following criteria: age of house, type of house (terraced, semi-detached, flat, etc), size of house (in rooms) and whether they were council, privately rented or owner occupied areas. Some might have gone so far as to describe housing as being 'middle-class semi-detached', for example. This exercise does highlight several factors. First, there is a tendency to identify social groups in the city from the external visual image of the houses. Second, such external assessments based on quality of upkeep, building style and so on do not necessarily tell us about the inhabitants and they are based on our cultural preconceptions. How can we tell that inhabitants are working class because they live on a council estate, when so many council houses are being sold? Likewise, how can we tell if an area is middle-class? Third, we do need to know why people choose to live where they do (that is assuming that they do have a real choice). Finally, we need to know about the processes influencing patterns of housing and social space which we identify accurately and perceive with varying degrees of accuracy.

Housing choice

The processes by which people come to select where they will live have been examined very closely in recent years. What has emerged is an increasing awareness of the interaction between environment and human behaviour. This link is not **deterministic**, ie. the environment will always predetermine certain responses. The relationship depends in a whole series of ways on the individual's response to an environment. Two basic factors do seem to underlie our patterns of housing choice. **life cycle** and **social class** or **life level**.

The concept of **life cycle** suggests that as we move through life so our housing needs change. Obviously the elderly widow and the family with three children, for example, have very little control over where they live, but home environments inevitably influence the housing aspirations or desires of the young on reaching adulthood. This happens because the home and school environments are major formers of the ideas, opinions and beliefs that we acquire during that stage of

socialisation; the process of being educated to be a member of a particular society. The second stage is a move to an independent unit as a single person. For some of you this might be a small rented flat which is also a rejection of the previous child-oriented life. This phase also includes communal dwelling in order to reduce rental costs and the growing practice of cohabitation outside marriage. This phase is of increasing importance now that the median interval between marriage and the first birth is 30 months compared with 20 months in 1971. It is 44 months for professional households. Marriage and the arrival of a family requires further relocation to appropriate environments, often involving several moves over the years. Finally, as the children leave and with the death of one partner, so there is a further potential for migration. It is the two person household at this stage and the earlier second stage in the cycle who comprise 1 in 3 households in the UK. Each of these stages produces a corresponding demand for housing which might be filled in the way suggested by Figure 5.1 and Table 5.1.

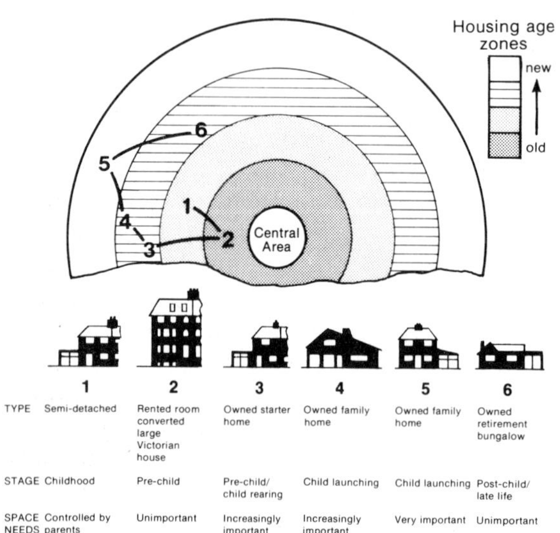

Figure 5.1 *Life cycle moves in a British city*

Table 5.1 **Household size in Great Britain 1961 and 1980**

Size	% 1961	No in millions	% 1980	No in millions
1 person	12	1.9	22	3.3
2 people	30	4.8	32	5.7
3 people	23	3.7	17	3.4
4 people	19	3.1	18	3.1
5 people	9	1.4	7	1.5
6 or more people	7	1.0	4	1.1
Average household size	3.09		2.68	

Study activity

Examine the table. Describe and account for the main changes in household size between 1961 and 1980.

The second factor is that of **social class, life level** or **socio-economic** group which is a measure based on one's income, wealth, education and occupation. In Britain the type of house occupied is generally related to socio-economic group. Rex and Moore in a study of Birmingham identified seven **housing classes** in British cities: (i) outright owners of large houses in desirable areas (ii) mortgage payers who own houses in desirable areas (iii) council housing tenants (iv) tenants in slum housing owned by councils (v) tenants in privately rented accommodation (vi) owners of houses bought with short term loans compelled to let rooms to meet repayments (vii) tenants of rooms in multiple occupancy dwellings or lodging houses. To these one might add (viii) owners and mortgage payers who have bought former council house. The way in which social class influences housing can be clearly seen in Table 5.2.

Study question

1 What changes have occurred in housing tenure for the various social groups since 1961?

These two basic factors therefore affect an individual's home location. If we

Table 5.2 **Social class and type of housing tenure 1961 and 1976**

(LA = local authority)	Social Class	Owner Occupation Outright/with Mortgage 1976	%	1961	Public renting LA 1976	%	1961	Private renting 1976	%	1961
Professionals, employers and managers	1	80		67	7		7	12		26
Intermediate non-manual	2	70		60	12		11	18		28
Skilled non-manual	3	55		51	25		17	20		32
Skilled manual	4	50		40	37		29	13		31
Semi-skilled manual	5	34		29	47		32	19		39
Unskilled manual	6	23		22	61		39	16		39

assume that people do move house, those in Rex and Moore's groups (iv) to (vi) generally move to (ii) and (iii) and some from (iii) move to the new group (viii) which is a subdivision of (ii). We see (i), (ii) and (viii) as desirable situations in a property owning democracy and (iii)/(iv) as part of our welfare state, whereas (vi) and (vii) are seen as undesirable. Both the **life cycle** and **socio-economic** group have been incorporated in Figure 5.2, which enables mobility to be related to the structure models of Mann and Robson discussed in Chapter 2.

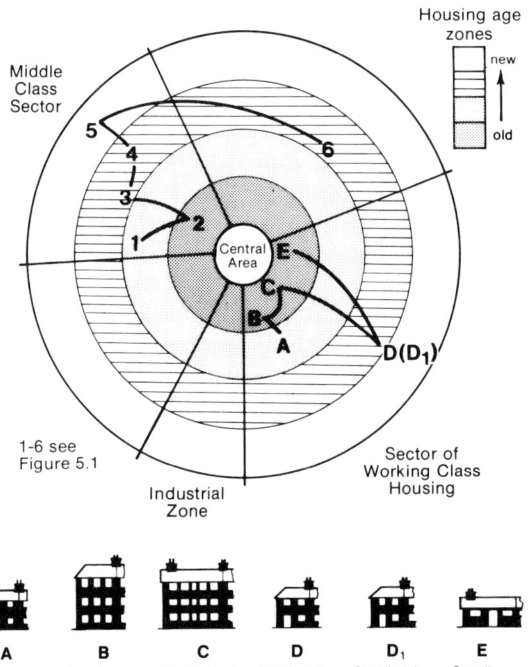

Figure 5.2 *Contrasting life cycle and social housing moves in a British city*

In addition to these two processes one must add the process of **filtering** which is the way by which existing housing stock is adapted over the years to supply the subsequent demands which we noted in Chapter 4. It takes the simple form illustrated in Figure 5.3 as new housing is built for each new higher income group and the housing which these groups vacate is then occupied by the next lower income group. However, there is also a process by which some of the original low income housing close to the city centre or in a unique situation becomes socially desirable and is socially upgraded. This process is known as **gentrification** and is stage iv on Figure 5.3. This happened in Chelsea some time ago and is now occurring in Islington.

> **Study activity**
>
> 1 Do you know of any area that has been **gentrified**?
> 2 Can you say why this has occurred; was it the type of house, the location, fashion or any other factor which sparked off the process?

Over half the house purchasers in Great Britain move less than 5 miles and under 10% over 50 miles, which suggests that we should regard housing choice and mi-

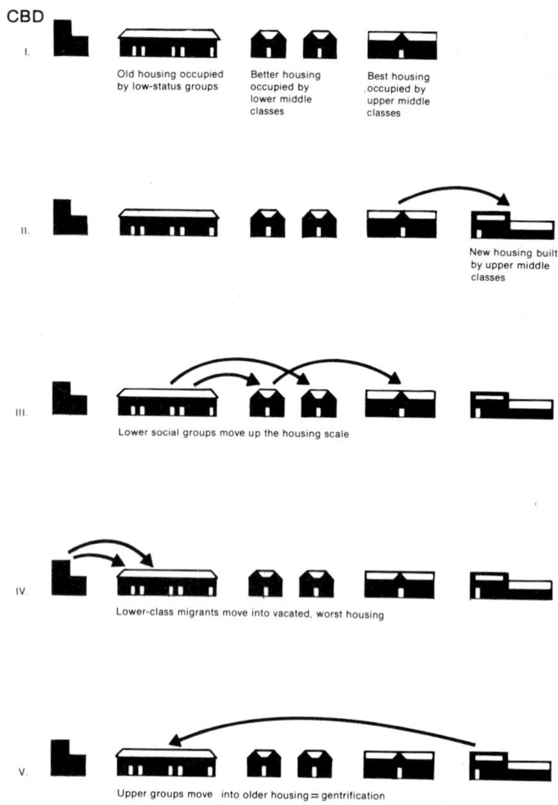

Figure 5.3 *Filtering*

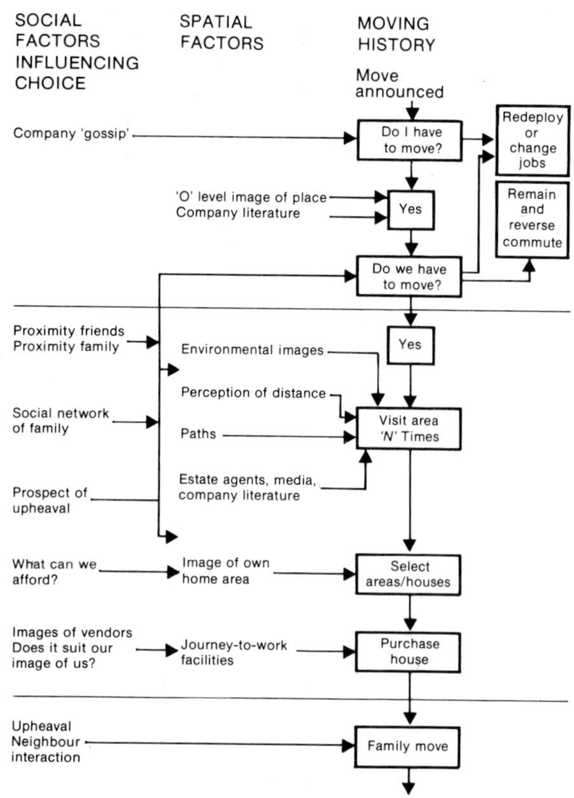

Figure 5.4 *Residential choice pattern for migrants to Portsmouth 1969–1976*

gration of households in a city as an important factor in the formation of the social areas of a city. Studies of residential choice have focussed both on moves between and within cities although the results do show similar factors influencing choice. In a six year study of the moves of office workers from London to Portsmouth, the pattern of residential selection shown in Figure 5.4 occurred. The employees were given copious help in the form of company information and estate agents' literature which enabled them to assess areas and houses in terms of their own existing and previous homes and other environmental influences.

A much more sophisticated model used by Brown and Moore does elaborate the rather simple study of movement to Portsmouth (Figure 5.5). The decision to move is based on factors internal and external to the family which build up to force a decision which they termed the conversion from **stress** to **strain**. The decision or strain is taken and if they decide to relocate then they go through a set process until they find a home or abandon the search and remain where they are. This model emphasises personal choice although the factors which might force the family to give up searching may have nothing to do with choice. They might find that the house which they need and want is beyond their pocket. Alternatively there are many households for whom the whole concept of choice is meaningless.

Study questions

1 For whom might the concept of housing choice be relatively meaningless?
2 Assume that you had to leave home now (or move if you are a mature student) what constraints would there be on your choice?

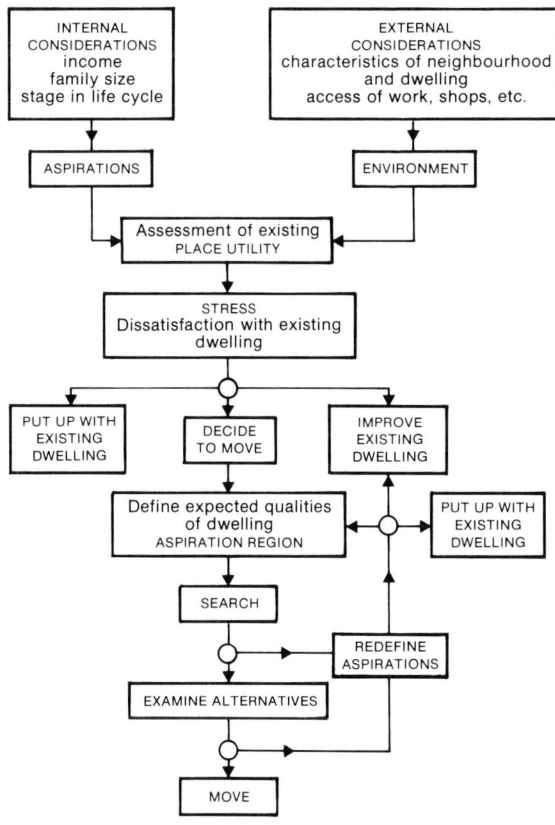

Figure 5.5 Brown and Moore's model of housing choice

Choice among council tenants

Studies which have been made of the housing preferences of council house tenants do suggest that their 'choices' are very different from the mortgaged owner occupier. In two case studies of requests to move made by council tenants in Newcastle and London it was shown that large numbers of people wish to move but are unable to do so. Moves are generally within a single local authority area because swaps between areas are very complicated to arrange. In London 44% of the tenants wished to move out from the inner estates to those nearer the fringe of the GLC area and beyond. Moves are generally requested to houses rather than flats. In contrast, the general pattern of transfer requests in Newcastle was towards the centre. The lack of shopping facilities in some of the outer estates together with poor public transport access and the strong community spirit of the inner areas were all seen as possible explanations for this pattern of choices. People on the west of the city remained firmly on that side and people from the east rarely asked to cross the city. This tendency to select only from one area of the city is common to owner occupiers as well and shows how limited is our knowledge of a city. There is now a government scheme to help council tenants to move from one city to another which was difficult in the past and acted as a brake on the mobility of tenants.

Choice and competition for scarce housing

Another example of the lack of choice that exists for some sections of society has been studied in Brighton. Here it was found that 5500 students of the University and Polytechnic live in 1600 privately rented households and that these households are in direct competition with low income households for rented accommodation. Student accommodation has been gaining at the expense of the low income groups because students are transient. They move on and so do not wish for security of tenure which the 1974 Rent Act has given. Students can group together to pay rents which low income families cannot do and so the student demand and choice can be satisfied. The students can gain access to houses with 4–6 rooms which are designed for a family, but the students can afford the rent because they have more contributors to the rent than the family with only one breadwinner.

Access to housing

There are, therefore, various **housing submarkets**, some of which are in competition with one another like the students and low income families. The choice is constrained and the constraints are operated by **gatekeepers**. These are the various institutions and their representatives who can constrain choice. Estate agents, landlords, property developers, banks, building societies, the local authority housing department and central government through the Department of

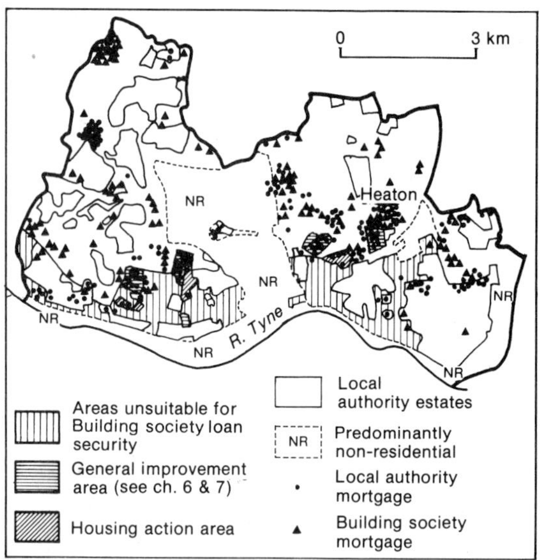

Figure 5.6 Mortgage patterns in Newcastle

the Environment are all gatekeepers. Let us look at how some of these work.

The building societies, banks and finance companies together with the assistance of estate agents, solicitors and mortgage brokers all help to allocate housing. They use invested money to lend to prospective buyers and so they have to be sure that the investors' money is reasonably safely used. In assessing whether I can buy a particular house, a building society considers my level of income and that of my wife, together with our financial prospects. They take account of age, marital status and size of family. These socio-economic characteristics will determine how much you can borrow and for how long. Secondly, the characteristics of the house, such as age, location, type and state of repair are considered. The general result is that middle class, male-headed families, and predominantly white families, gain access to owner occupied housing depending on how much they have invested in another house or saved up for a deposit. The poor, the elderly, single parents and some ethnic minorities are excluded from owner occupation. Another constraint which existed until 1977 was a practice known as **red lining**. Areas were designated as unsuitable for loans by building societies. Whole areas of inner cities were excluded from mortgages thus forcing those who wanted to live there to obtain loans at much higher interest rates. Local authorities in England and Wales did try to bridge this gap by lending to people who wished to live in older property or who were lower income or first time buyers. This source of finance fell away dramatically after 1976 with successive public spending cuts. Even estate agents have been known to keep like with like and deter the unlike persons from moving in. Thus the Asian community in Leicester has developed its own network of estate agents obviously to counteract the former bias of the agents.

A study of patterns of mortgage finance in Newcastle-upon-Tyne illustrates how local authority and building society mortgages did show evidence of being clustered in different areas. Figure 5.6 shows how local authority finance was concentrated into the areas receiving other help to improve the environment, whereas the building societies preferred different suburban locations and only in the Heaton area did they invest in the improvement areas.

Access to council housing is controlled by a different set of gatekeepers. Formally, to gain access to a council house a person or family had to live in the area; the law changed this requirement in 1980. Some authorities only accepted an aplicant if their income was low. Frequently the applicant

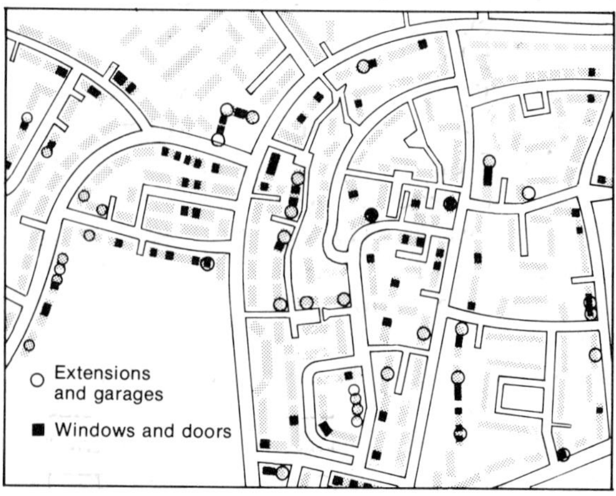

Figure 5.7 The evidence of council house sales, Leigh Park

Table 5.3 Status of tenant and property type in Hull Council Houses (after Gray)

	Local Authority Opinion of Tenant		
	Poor/Fair	Fairly good/Good	Very good/Excellent
Percentage of tenants occupying dwellings built			
1919–1944	62.5	13.9	10.7
1945–1965	29.2	38.0	28.6
1965–1974	8.3	23.4	17.9
New in 1975	—	24.7	42.8
Average rateable value	£176.70	£201.90	£209.90

was given points to determine the priority of his/her need, such as medical need, overcrowding and present housing. Homelessness enables one to 'jump the queue' for placement. None of the decisions are made available to applicants. In the past authorities tended to group 'good' tenants based on rent paying promptness and 'problems' so that the social groups were segregated with the 'worst' tenants found in 'dust-bin', poor quality estates, often built before 1939, or in the less desirable parts of the council's property. In this way areas were labelled as bad, almost as a direct result of decisions by bureaucratic gatekeepers. In Hull, for example, a housing investigator completed a form taking details and even inspecting the rent book. In 1972 a random selection of additional comments assessing households revealed how important these gatekeepers are in deciding who goes where. Comments included, 'Excellent tenant, suitable for new property', 'Good type of OAP, suitable for new or post-war re-let' and 'Fair only – suitable for pre-war property'. Table 5.3 shows a distinct relationship between age of property, its rateable value and the quality of the tenant. Low status households are disadvantaged and are more and more trapped in low status property. By paying rents standardised for size of properties they are also subsidising the tenants in new accommodation of the same size.

An alternative way of looking at these constraints is the division between **dominant groups**, those exercising control over the allocation of resources and affecting the life changes of others, and **muted groups**, those whose interests are not fully appreciated. The latter could be children, racial minorities or single parent families who find that the city's housing is structured in the interests of the dominant group, thus supressing the muted groups' activities. Lack of play space, absence of crêches and lack of cultural facilities for minorities are examples of how muted groups are constrained from moving into certain areas of the city.

Study activity

Who are the gatekeepers for the rented properties which were sought after by students and the lower paid in Brighton?

More recently it has been the policy of both central (Conservative) government and many local government authorities to sell council houses to tenants because, in the words of a 1977 government report, home ownership is 'basic and natural'. The effect of this can be seen in Figure 5.7 where the location of sold homes is based on visual evidence gathered in the field. The sold properties cluster in the better areas of this huge estate while there are other areas where no sales have taken place. These are the areas of poorer environmental quality and, perhaps, those tenants who cannot afford even these cut price sales. While these sales might benefit the new owners and save public money, there are losers, those on the waiting list who want council housing.

Study activity

What problems might follow later for the families who have bought their own homes in the council estates? Debate the pros and cons of council house sales. (This does require you to have opinions and to know why you hold these opinions.)

The product of the patterns of behaviour constrained by the institutions involved in housing has produced a pattern of changing desirability of areas and a pattern of socio-spatial segregation. Higher income groups have tended to leave the city. The older housing is technologically obsolete. Where is the space for freezers or dishwashers, or for a laundry room or second bathroom? Where is the space for the second car? There are **negative externalities** which follow on from the loss of certain groups of people: such as poorer schools, increasing crime, cut-backs of public services and the lowering socio-economic status of those who remain. In 1981–1982 the Toxteth area of Liverpool was highlighted in this way, first by riots and then by a report which emphasised the negative externalities of the area.

On the other hand, areas can move up-market as we saw with gentrification in Islington. Good quality recent housing developments are labelled as 'desirable' by estate agents and so their prices inflate more rapidly. This can be the result of location or popularity evident in the speed of sales in an area.

Study activity

Draw a map of the 'desirable' and 'less desirable' residential areas in your vicinity. How did you decide on 'desirability'? What is the evidence for your conclusions?

Housing and social segregation – the ghetto

Perhaps the most extreme case of social segregation which manifests itself today is that of the segregation of many of the New Commonwealth immigrants in our cities. In their more extreme form these areas, particularly those housing coloured immigrants, have come to be called **ghettos**. The ghetto was the quarter of the medieval city reserved for the Jews and takes its name from *Geto* in Venice. It implies an extreme degree of segregation produced by a variety of forces. South African cities are, without doubt, the most rigidly segregated, although most developed western countries do seem to show some measure of ethnic and cultural segregation.

A study of the coloured population in Birmingham based on the 1961 and 1971 census has shown how those classified by the census as New Commonwealth (Indian, Pakistan, Bangladeshi and West Indian) have concentrated their residences in distinct parts of the city. In 1961 most West Indian districts had only 36% of residents born in the West Indies, whereas by 1971 61% had been born there. The main areas were to the north and

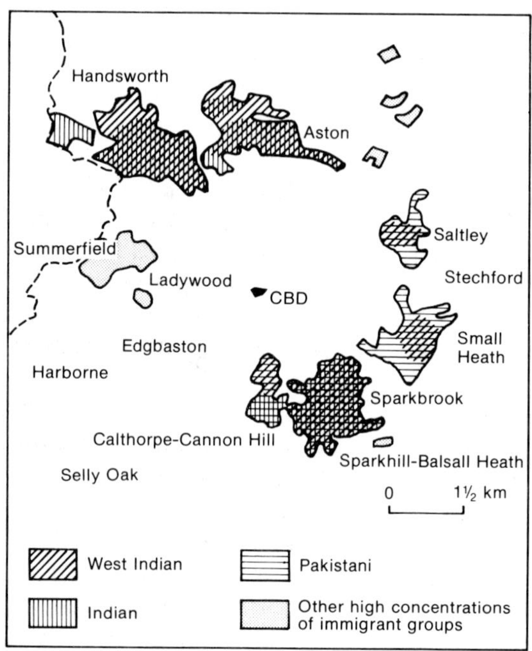

Figure 5.8 Immigrant housing areas in Birmingham

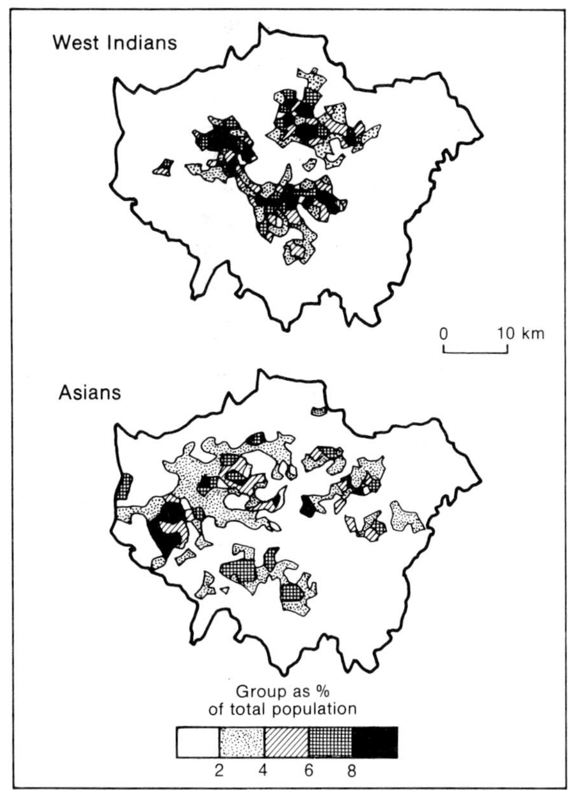

Figure 5.9 *Residential patterns of West Indians and Asians in London 1971*

west of the centre in areas of multiple occupancy of lodging houses or poor quality housing, such as Sparkbrook and Handsworth. The Indians, Pakistanis and Bangladeshis occupy other areas of the city (Figure 5.8) which have taken on certain of the cultural attributes of those societies.

The maps of residential patterns of West Indians and Asians in London (Figure 5.9) also show distinct concentrations. The Bengali groups have concentrated in the East End which has had a long tradition of immigration. Here the Huguenot (French protestant) church, which became a Jewish synagogue and then a Muslim temple, graphically illustrates this tradition. West Indian concentrations in Brixton and Notting Hill have received much attention in the media, as has the Indian community in Southall. At a more detailed level it has been noted that the immigrants from the different West Indian islands cluster in separate parts of the West Indian areas.

There are seveal reasons for ethnic residential clusters which can be classified as defensive, avoidance, preservation and attack functions all deriving from a feeling of conflict between the host population and the immigrants. By joining an ethnic cluster it is possible to reduce one's own feeling of isolation and provides some form of security. This is a **defensive** reaction which is not only found among coloured populations. In Belfast and Londonderry the concentrations of religious protagonists into segregated areas is a case in point. Similarly the Bengali group in the Spitalfields district of East London concentrated in a smaller area and asked for police protection when faced with threats from the National Front.

By concentrating, **avoidance** of outside contact can be maintained and the group can support its members. In such an area a Mosque, shops and services which specialise in serving a particular community's needs can easily develop. Later immigrants then have a stable environment to enter in the host country where traditions are preserved. **Preservation** of identity and promotion of one's own cultural heritage is important. Indians and Pakistanis have distinct language, religious and social organisations and therefore have a strong wish to remain independent. The author has come across cases of girls from an ethnic minority unable to undertake 'A' level geography projects outside school because of the resistance to their mixing without strict parental supervision. The need to preserve a strong culture has been less manifest among the West Indians, although the rise of Rastafarian culture is an attempt to develop a stronger West Indian identity.

The ethnic concentration is also a means by which action against society in general can be based. This **attack** function can be peaceful or, as we have witnessed in recent years in St Pauls (Bristol), Brixton, Moss Side and Toxteth, more violent.

Whether the concentrations of ethnic groups in British cities warrant the use of the term ghetto is a matter of debate. They are small in scale compared with those in the United States where the size and rate of spread of the Atlanta Ghetto provides a graphic example of the problem (Figure 5.10). Nevertheless, a city like Belfast does have large, segregated Roman Catholic areas which have expanded outwards in a sectoral fashion. Also ethnic concentrations in British cities have lower proportions of minority groups, although this depends very much on the scale of the area of measurement. In Glasgow, Asians rarely form more than 40% of households in an area although a set of appartments might be totally Asian.

While colour might seem to be the most common basis of ethnic segregation in Britain, the USA and South Africa, language, religion and national origins will often form the basis elsewhere. In Canada, which prides itself on being a **multicultural** society, almost every city has concentrations of the multitude of cultural groups that make up the modern Canadian population. In Toronto, French, Poles, Italians, Jews, Ukranians and, more recently, Vietnamese, all have distinct areas of town (Figure 5.11). In some cities other minorities flourish, preserving their culture and tradition by concentrating in parts of the city. Kitchener-Waterloo has a significant German minority which is unique in Canada. Admittedly greater integration has taken place but more recently efforts have been made, not as a result of defence, to rekindle the appreciation of the cultures

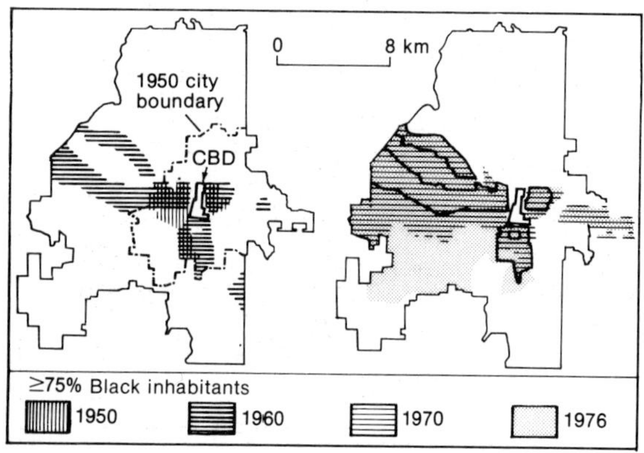

Figure 5.10 The growth of the Atlanta Ghetto

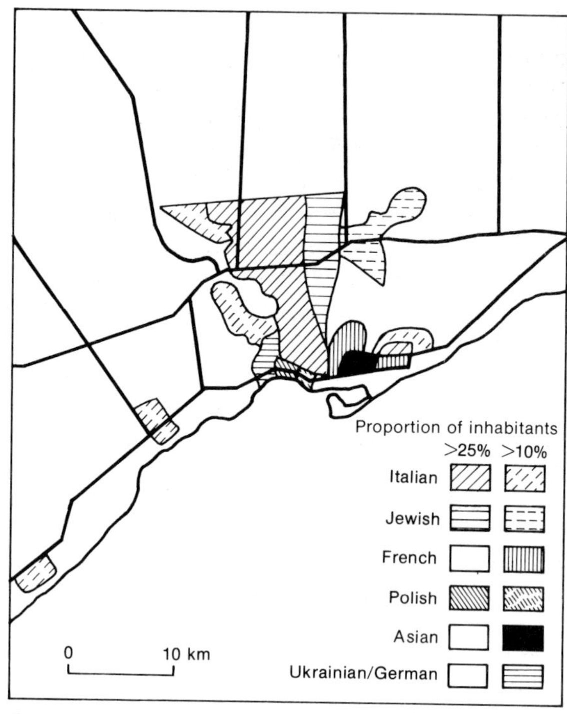

Figure 5.11 Cultural groups in Toronto

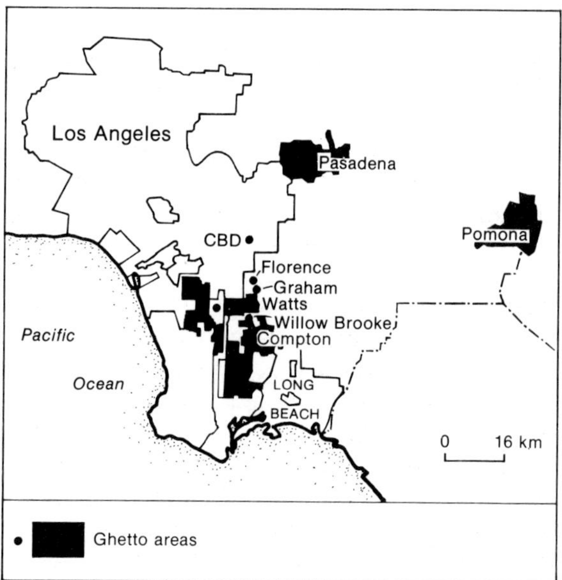

Figure 5.12 The Los Angeles ghetto areas

that make up Canadian cities and perhaps segregation will be reinforced.

The ghetto in the USA has a much longer history. Ghettos were recognisable as such before the 1920s in Atlanta, Baltimore,

Chicago and New York. Others have appeared since in almost every city. The areas which the negro population have occupied have remained relatively permanent because of restrictive housing policies and unwritten discriminatory practices such as only selling houses in black or white areas to the same racial group. Nevertheless, the sheer size of the black population in some cities such as Washington DC and Detroit, which are respectively 74% and 44% black, has resulted in a suburbanisation process among the black population. Much of this takes the form of **spillover**, the gradual suburban spread of the ghetto area. In other instances areas that were once shanty settlements beyond the urban fringe but on the railroads have become engulfed by sprawl and become permanent black suburbs. In other cases **leapfrogging** has taken place, the black population colonises an area of white suburbia which often comprises apartment blocks and spreads from that new core. In Los Angeles the core of the ghetto is Watts and this has spread to Compton, Willowbrook, Florence and Graham (Figure 5.12). On the other hand, in Passadena Pomona the ghetto is far out into the urban fringe. Spatial segregation of the black residential areas indicates increasing segregation within that community.

Study questions

1 Is ethnic segregation an inevitable process?
2 How can ethnic segregation be reduced?
3 Should ethnic segregation be reduced?
When answering these questions ask yourself why you hold your particular opinions and where the ideas and opinions originated.

Social segregation – patterns of crime and deviance

For several years now various geographers have become aware of concentrations of

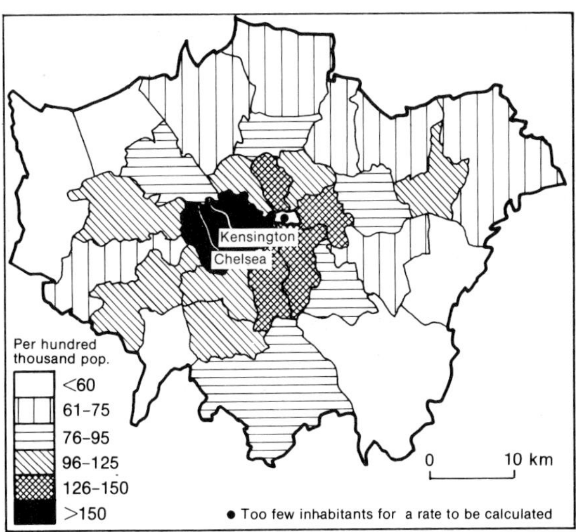

Figure 5.13 Distribution of patients admitted to psychiatric hospitals suffering from schizophrenia in London 1976

other social phenomena in cities. Even Burgess noted vice and underworld on his model of Chicago. In the 1950s a study of Liverpool noted that the handicapped and the mentally ill were concentrated towards the centre of the city. Schizophrenia patients in London are much more concentrated in boroughs such as Kensington and Chelsea (Figure 5.13) and other inner boroughs. In contrast, suicides are found more in the affluent inner areas. Inner areas have larger concentrations of the divorced, widowed, the

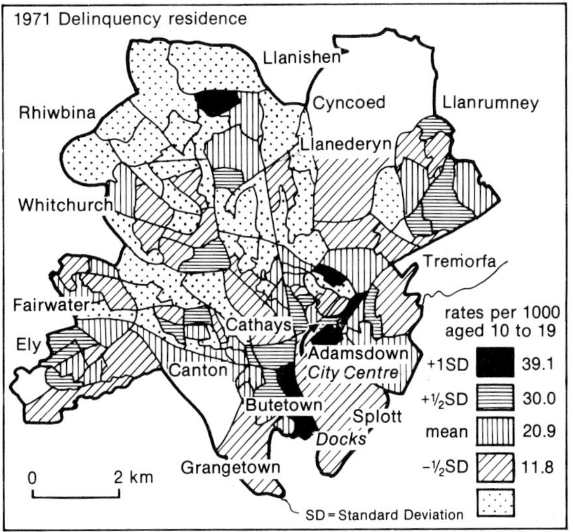

Figure 5.14 Delinquency areas in Cardiff 1971

single parent family and the elderly.

A study of delinquency in Cardiff in 1971 (Figure 5.14) does show very distinct clusters of delinquency residences. The work goes on to suggest that in the areas of delinquency residences there is a subculture which, perhaps like the ghetto, binds a social group together and produces a **neighbourhood effect** recognised both by those who live there and by outsiders. Little evidence exists to show that it is the environment which determines a deviant sub-culture, rather it is attributed to the social characteristics of the group and their attitudes towards education, crime and punishment. Thus while certain environments in the inner city and council estates might appear to have concentrations of deviant behaviour, it is the characteristics of the people and not the building styles which are the root cause. It might also be that studies have concentrated on crimes where the success rate among the police is high avoiding 'middle-class' crimes which may be harder to detect and which are infrequently taken to the courts. Tax evasion is one such crime where only a small proportion reach the courts and it is a crime of the better-off. Similarly fraud and embezzlement cases are the crimes of the well-to-do which would show a very different pattern.

With our ageing population, the housing of the elderly is an important topic for the future.

Study activity

Prepare a map of the distribution of facilities for the elderly in a town. Can you offer any explanation for the distribution?

Housing in socialist states – the USSR

Between 1960 and 1975 two thirds of the population of the USSR were rehoused and so the major parts of Soviet cities now comprise housing layouts preferred by the central authorities. The basic unit of housing policy is the **mikrorayon** which is the housing and associated functions for a population of

Figure 5.15 The mikrorayon

8–12 000 people. These are aggregated into groups of 4 or 5 mikrorayons to form a **residential complex** with its open space, child care facilities, schools, health services and old peoples' home. The typical outline of such a complex is shown in Figure 5.15. The mikrorayon itself comprises a set of smaller living complexes or **qvartal**.

Housing quality and space per person has risen steadily in the socialist states. While the space per person is small by our standards the allocation is more equitable. Nevertheless, certain privileged elites do receive special attention and, despite attempts to mix society within the mikrorayon, there is evidence that some groups do concentrate in certain areas of the town. However, the USSR has gone a long way to achieving social justice in housing everyone according to their need, which is in sharp contrast with other states. Against this must be set the fact that the conditions of daily life in the suburbs of the USSR are still deficient. Shopping and transport difficulties loom large.

The housing problem in third world cities

In Chapter 1 we looked at the effect of over-rapid urbanisation on cities in the third world and the growth of **spontaneous settlements**.

Table 5.4 Spontaneous settlements

Name	Country	City	Example
Barriadas	Peru	Lima	Comas, St Martin
Barrioclanesino	Colombia	Bogota	Barrio of 65; El Carmen
Favela	Brazil	Rio de Janiero	
Bidonville	Iraq	Baghdad	Asima
Bidonville	Morocco	Casablanca	
Gourbivilles	Tunisia	Tunis	Djebel Lahmar
Shanty Town	Zambia	Lusaka	
Callampas	Chile	Santiago	
Colonias populares	Mexico	Mexico City	Ecatepec
Barong-barong	Philippines		Tondo
Bustee	India	Calcutta	(See Figure 5.17)
Squatter settlement	Hong Kong	———	Diamond Hill
Gecekondu	Turkey	Istanbul	
Ranchos	Venezuela	Caracas	Petare

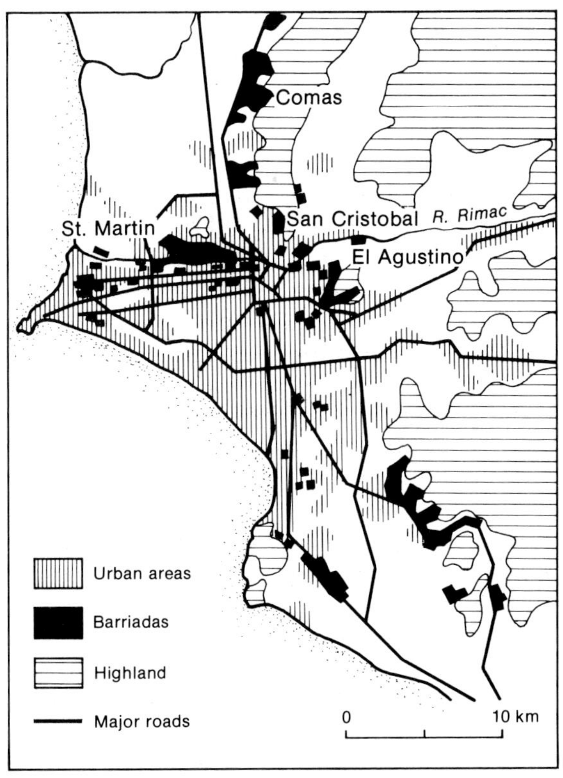

Figure 5.16 The barriadas of Lima

Spontaneous settlements have been a continuing feature of third world cities for well over a century, and references to them can be found in the history of development of most cities. Table 5.4 gives a list of some of the terms used to refer to spontaneous settlements. Figure 5.16 shows the location of the barriadas in Lima. Here the spontaneous settlement accounted for 40% of the total population and 80% of the growth of the city between 1961 and 1971. Estimates for 1990 suggest that 4.5 million people will live in the barriadas. These are in small patches near the centre which are the most chaotic. North-east of the city are some larger areas of barriadas along the steep hills. More recently new barriadas have grown around the industrial areas, the port and up to 15 km out to the south-east. These areas are in marked contrast to the more westernised areas of housing with their lower densities, proper sanitation and air of affluence.

The bustees of Calcutta represent a stage up from the most severe housing problems of all in third world cities, those people who had no shelter and live on the pavements (there were 100000 as long ago as 1966). There are over 3000 separate bustees in Calcutta with some of the worst living conditions in the world (Figure 5.17) where cholera, smallpox and tuberculosis are normal hazards. They have been seen as a cancerous growth by middle class Indians but others see them as the most natural way of housing a vast urban poor when public finance is not available for rehousing. Public investment has been concentrated on sanitation, water supply and basic environmental improvements so that local trades could flourish and permanent dwellings might succeed the ramshackle tin, wood, mud and even cardboard huts. The solution in Lima has been similar; self-help and minimal government assistance, have resulted in some areas becoming more permanent. Permanence of dwellings is usually associated with the upper strata of the Peruvian poor, the **consolidators** or those who have made some progress despite the harsh realities of life in a third world city.

There are other more drastic responses to spontaneous settlements. In Caracas and Hong Kong high rise, high density apartment blocks have been constructed; although in the case of Caracas the pace of building has never kept up with the flow of immigrants from the ranchos, and so more and more poorly built settlements grow up in the ravines. In contrast the number of urban squatters in Hong Kong has diminished in the face of a vast government programme which has been aided by the rapid economic growth of the colony. On the other hand, little or no help has been given to the spontaneous settlements so that people are encouraged to move to the new, cheaply constructed high-rise blocks rather than live in the spartan conditions of the squatter settlement. The recent influx of Vietnamese boat people is a further pressure which the government has to face.

Both Hong Kong and Venezuela have also used high density new settlements (**new towns**) to house the urban migrants. Hong

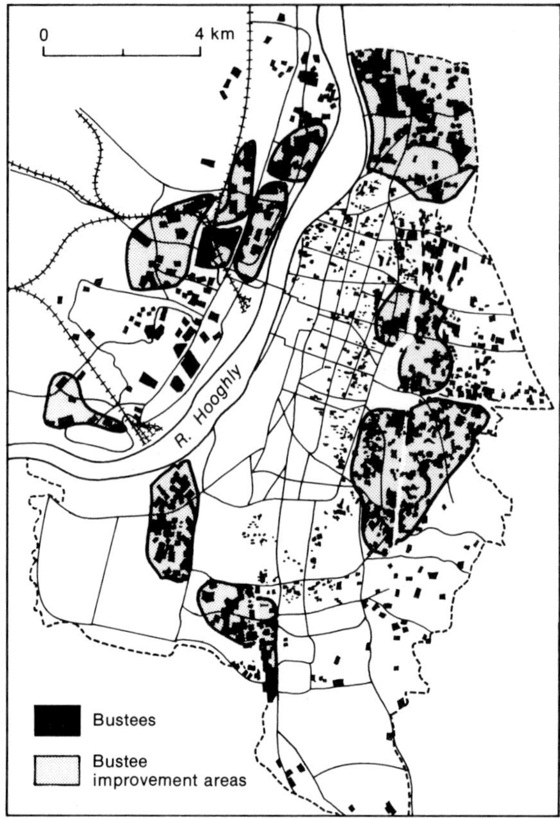

Figure 5.17 The bustees of Calcutta

Kong has built two at Tsuen Wan and Kwun Tong in the New Territories to house approximately 300000 people. Venezuela developed Cuidad Guyana as a new growth point on the Orinoco to help steer the flow of migrants away from the developed coastal belt. Other new towns are under development outside Caracas and Maracaibo in association with major industrial developments.

A third compromise solution to the housing problems of the third world's poor has been attempted in Zambia. Here **site and service schemes** have been tried. The state provides basic facilities and the foundation for houses and then permits the occupier to construct his dwelling as and how he wishes. Even those schemes are thwarted by the inability of governments to pay for the basic sanitary requirements and for the expensive waste disposal systems that are needed.

Housing and social conditions in much

Study activity

Professor Dwyer made this plea. Why is housing in third world cities so difficult to improve?
'Must increasing numbers of urban families in the third world be condemned to such levels of existence? In an age when man has reached the moon, surely not'.

of the third world do appear to represent a more polarised version of the divides which affect housing provision and the social geography of western cities. Is it that by copying the West that the new states have created these housing problems which they cannot solve? Would it be possible to develop a socialist third world housing policy or does cost also rule this out? Could and should the developed world provide aid, know-how and expertise to help overcome the problems of spontaneous housing?

Conclusion

At the beginning of this chapter we asked you to map the housing areas of a town or city and since then we have tried to examine the factors which might account for the patterns of housing and social groups that we can see in cities in Britain and elsewhere. Much more emphasis was placed on our explanations of human behaviour and the spatial outcomes of that behaviour. People have constrained choices and other people can modify choice by their decisions. Nevertheless, decisions about where to live are constrained by the availability of information.

In drawing your map of residential areas you were no doubt constrained by the information available to you at that time. Your map based on your memory or **mental map** was no doubt of a variable and highly inaccurate scale. It contained more detail on the areas you know and ignored other districts. Your mental map serves to underline one aspect of modern geography and that is the relevance of understanding the aggregate behaviour of individuals. Behaviour in housing choice or reactions to labels for areas are partly influenced by our own socialisation, aspirations and our values.

Certain of the discussions that you might have had concerning ghettos, the sale of council houses and spontaneous housing did not have easy answers because different opinions and values were expressed. Another characteristic of modern geography enables us to look at what people value or believe and how this might affect our towns and cities. The encouragement of owner occupation, house buying and council house sales represents one set of values or perhaps an **ideology** (system of beliefs). Increased state involvement in housing and land ownership, and efforts to equalise opportunities in housing represent another ideology. Therefore the social geography of a city or town cannot be viewed from a neutral standpoint because we have values and we are studying the good and bad effects on the built environment of values held by people and politicians.

Revision

Finally, by way of revision, can you answer some of the following?

1 What do you understand by the following concepts:
- the life cycle
- socialisation
- filtering
- negative externalities
- values
- ideology.

2 Who are gatekeepers, consolidators, muted groups?

3 What is
- (i) a site and service scheme
- (ii) an enumeration district
- (iii) a mikrorayon
- (iv) a barriadas
- (v) red lining

4 Why do people move house?

5 Why do people segregate into distinct social areas?

6

Responding to urban growth

The last two chapters have outlined the variety of ways in which cities and towns have spread and the social and economic problems that are emerging. Whether we like or dislike the effects of growth depends very much on our own values. In this section we can turn to the ways in which our society has responded to the issue of rapid urban growth. The response has been channelled through the agency of the planning profession in which high hopes were placed ever since Town and Country Planning was first introduced into this country. Over the last fifty years government influence on the growth of cities has increased. This chapter will look both at the legislation and the products of that legislation to control growth.

Reacting to growth

The initial reactions to the nineteenth century growth of cities were a concern for the health hazards of our urban areas. Despite early legislation to control the most insalubrious urban conditions real control over urban growth did not materialise until we were aware of the rate at which urban growth was consuming valuable rural land at the fringe. In the 1930s this reached 60000 acres per year for both housing and new decentralised industrial estates such as Park Royal in West London or Slough further west along the Great West Road. Witton Park, Birmingham and Trafford Park, Manchester date from the same period.

Similar concerns have been expressed over the years in almost all developed countries. In the rapidly growing area of Main Street, Canada (see Chapter 1), it has been calculated that 183 acres of land are needed for every 1000 people and in the United States the figure of 220 acres per thousand has been calculated. All too frequently, as in Britain, many of the cities are sprawling across some of the best agricultural land.

The reaction to urbanisation and urban sprawl was led from the turn of the century in Britain by Ebenezer Howard's **garden city movement**. It was an anti-urban movement to combat the worst excesses of the nineteenth century that proposed self-contained and self-sustaining cities of 30000 people, so stopping the growth of existing towns. As a result an agglomeration of garden cities would be the essence of his **social city**. Two garden cities were started at Letchworth (1903) and Welwyn Garden City (1920). In the first forty years of the present century other prototype urban planners began to formulate ideas and to translate Howard's ideas to reality. Parker and Unwin, who had designed Letchworth, built Hampstead Garden Suburb and later Parker designed the Wythenshawe area of Manchester. By 1915 Patrick Geddes developed a theory of planning and the now well known sequence of (i) survey (ii) analyse the survey (iii) plan. Sir Patrick Abercrombie, the founder of the Council for the Preservation of Rural England, was developing ideas for controlled suburban growth which were to emerge after 1940 in his plans for Greater London, Glasgow, and Birmingham. Outside Britain other architect planners were developing ideas. In the United States the idea of the distinct, inward looking **neighbourhood** was developed by Perry, while Stein with the now famous **Radburn layout**, introduced the concept of segregation of pedestrians from motor traffic as early as 1933. In France the architect Le Corbusier was designing new urban forms for high density cities in the form of extremely tall skyscrapers. These developments were to feature in British cities after 1945.

Until the 1930s, despite the activities of the urban visionaries, the official reactions in Britain to the problems of urban expansion were very muted. The Town Planning Acts that had been passed in 1909, 1925 and 1932 were voluntary and gave no powers to stop development. The first real controls came in 1935 with powers to prevent **ribbon development** along major roads and in 1938 when the Green Belt Act enabled the creation of London's green belt. The depression years of the 1920s and 1930s also created a climate of opinion that was more prepared to accept many of the post-1945 proposals for control of city growth. In 1935 the Marley Report recommended garden city development. In 1940 the Barlow Report on the location of the industrial population dealt with a variety of topics beyond our scope here, but it did recommend controls of industrial location and a system of town and country planning. The Reith Committee (1946) recommended new towns as a part of the planned decentralisation of London and supported Abercrombie's principles for the dispersal of a million Londoners into ten satellite towns. Tables 6.1 and 6.2 provide a summary of the major reports and Acts or Parliament from this time to the present that illustrate how much government control has developed in the past half century.

The development of urban planning in Britain

The 1947 Town and Country Planning Act

This act is the foundation of all subsequent urban planning. It enabled local authorities to develop land and to have total control over development. It also enabled **compulsory purchase** of land needed for public developments to be enforced. Local authorities were

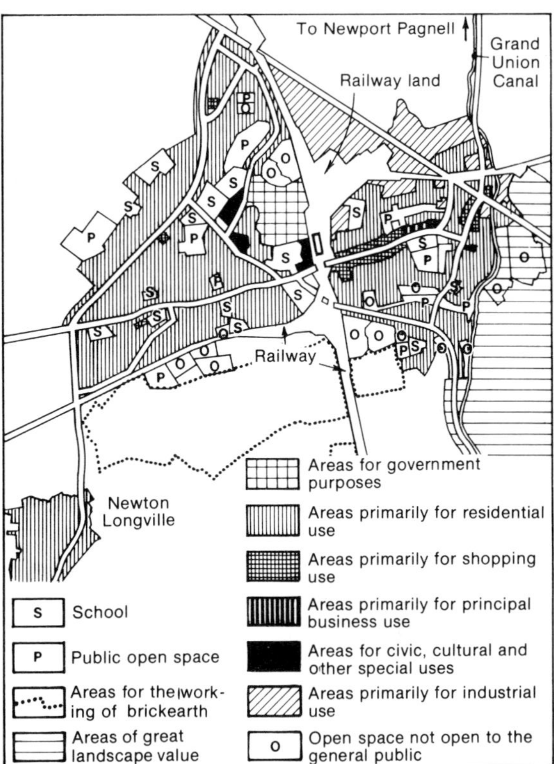

Figure 6.1 A development plan map of Bletchley

compelled to draw up a **development plan** and revise it every five years. The principles of the plan's preparation were to be those of Geddes. The plan would show all important developments and proposed land use changes for the next 20 years. Anyone who wanted to change the land or building use or develop land had to receive permission from the local authority. There was a right of appeal to the Minister. Local authorities now set about preparing Development Plans. An example of the type of plan is shown in Figure 6.1 for Bletchley which was later to form part of Milton Keynes.

New Towns Act 1946 and expanded towns

The passing of this act gave the responsibility for new towns designation to the Minister for Town and Country Planning (now the Minister for the Environment). Between 1946 and 1950, fourteen new towns were designated, of which eight were around London. Only two of the eight, Harlow and Stevenage, (the first to be designated), were identical to

Abercrombie's proposals. In 1952 the Town Development Act provided for other expansion agreements between the big cities and smaller towns. Among the largest of these have been agreements between Greater London and Andover, Basingstoke and Swindon. This type of arrangement is known as an **expanded town**.

Other government involvement in planning

Throughout the period from 1945 until 1979 government involvement in urban development and change has increased and some of the legislation and reports are tabulated in Tables 6.1 and 6.2. The new laws were particularly concerned with housing conditions and we shall return to some of these in Chapter 7. Transport proposals were also a focus of attention in the Buchanan Report (1963) on traffic in towns and the Smeed Report (1964) on road pricing. Many of the Acts of Parliament which were passed or repealed did respond to national needs but these were needs seen through the ideology of the Government in power. For instance the encouragement of council house sales since 1979 has been pursued more vigorously.

Study activity

Find out when the Conservative and Labour Governments were in power and see if any of the Acts in Table 6.2 represent each government's ideology as you see it.

Government involvement in urban development could also be indirect through the operation, extension and contraction of Industrial Development Certificates (IDCs) and Office Development Permits (ODPs) which sought to control the economic growth of the south-east and steer it to the regions. Economic and regional policies did have local urban effects. For instance the economic help to Liverpool in a development district was available in Wilmslow, which had an expanded town arrangement with Liverpool, and yet Wilmslow was not in a development area. Industrial growth took place west of Shrewsbury, just inside Wales, where grants were available rather than in the town. Governments have also produced a series of regional planning documents such as the South East Study (1964); South East Strategy (1967); and Wales: The Way Ahead (1967), all of which indicated the potential nature of urban expansion in the region. This type of planning is **indicative planning** because it suggested ways forward.

Planning since the 1968 Town and Country Planning Act

Twenty years after the 1947 Act the pace of change had altered and it was felt that detailed land-use proposals were far too inflexible. The new Town and Country Planning Act set up a new two tier planning system. At the upper level there was to be the **structure plan** which would outline the main proposals in a generalised fashion. These proposals have to receive Ministry approval. Structure Plans are a county responsibility and Figure 6.2 shows the structure plan for one metropolitan county, Manchester. It paints a broad picture, attempting to balance the region's resources in terms of the city and the large towns, which encourage growth with the social and economic problems of the city and towns. Therefore the map stresses existing retail centres and office development in cities, while housing needs are noted both on the edge of the built-up areas and in areas of the inner city. The central aim throughout the study was to improve the quality of life for all and so the retention of open land along the river valleys, the lowering of housing densities and new housing areas are all seen as part of the 'broad brush' approach to the future of Greater Manchester.

Study activity

Using your local library find out what the Structure Plan for your area states.

Table 6.1 Major government reports on planning

date	chairman/title	proposal
1935	Marley	Garden cities be adopted
1940	Barlow	Industrial decentralisation from London new towns
1944	Abercrombie	Greater London plan
1946	Reith	New towns be established
1963	Buchanan	Traffic in Towns study
1964	South East Study	First Regional plan
1965	Milner Holland	Housing in London
1969	Skeffington	Public participation in planning
1977	Department of the Environment	Policy for the inner cities

Table 6.2 Acts of Parliament having a direct effect on the urban environment

date	act	effect
1909	Town Planning Act	Power to authorise town planning schemes (voluntary only)
1919	Housing and Town Planning Act (Addison Act)	Council house building commences
1925	Town Planning Act	Separate planning (still voluntary) for housing
1932	Town Planning Act	
1935	Restriction of Ribbon Development Act	Outlawed ribbon development
1938	Green Belt Act	Instituted the London green belt
1946	New Towns Act	First eight new towns
1947	Town and Country Planning Act	Development plans, planning permission
1949	Housing Act	Improvement grants
1949	Special Roads Act	Motorway development sanctioned
1952	Town Development Act	Overspill arrangements – 'expanded towns'
1956	Clean Air Act	Reduces pollution – smoke control
1964	Housing Act	Housing improvement areas
1965	Control of Offices Act	Office Development Controls and Permits

Table 6.2 continued

date	act	effect
1966	Industrial Development Act	Reclamation of derelict land
1967	Civic Amenities Act	Protect areas of special architectural or historic interest; Conservation Areas
1968	Town and Country Planning Act	Development Planning Two tiers a) Structure Plans b) Local Plans plus Action Area and Subject Plans
1968	Race Relations Act	
1968	Urban Aid Act	Attack on points of deprivation
1968	Transport Act	Passenger transport authorities for cities
1969	Housing Act	General improvement Area (GIA)
1970		Department of Environment created
1971	Town and Country Planning Act	Protected historic buildings
1972	Local Government Act	New local government districts, counties and metropolitan counties
1972	Town and Country Planning Act	Structure Plans a county responsibility; Local Plans a joint district/county responsibility
1972	Town and Country Planning Act	Reforms Local Government for 1974
1974	Control of Pollution Act	Smoke Control Zones, Noise Abatement Zones
1974	Town and Country Amenities Act	Care of old buildings
1974	Housing Act	Housing Action Areas and Priority Neighbourhoods
1975	Community Land Act	To return development values to the community as a whole; repealed in 1980
1978	Inner Urban Areas Act	Assistance to industry – Industrial Improvement Areas: Partnership Areas and Programme Districts
1979		Location of Offices Bureau abolished
1980	Local Government Planning and Land Act	Dismantles the control of Structure (County) Plans over Local (District) Plans

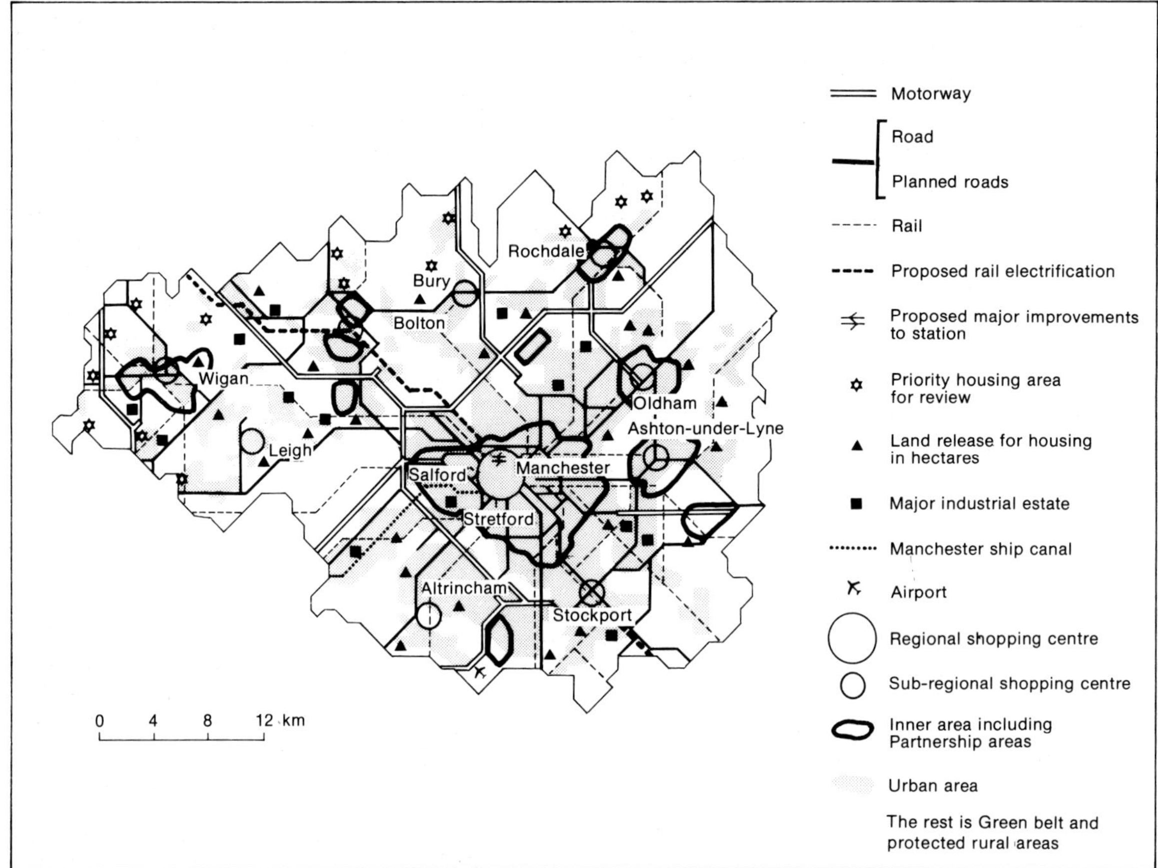

Figure 6.2 *The Greater Manchester structure plan*

Beneath the first tier of structure plans there are the **local plans** which are the joint responsibility of the districts and the county. These plans do not need ministerial approval, although in some cases, such as hypermarket developments, there is the potential for central government to alter plans and decisions.

The other aspect of these changes was that **public participation** was encouraged in the planning process, that is, 'the act of sharing in the formulation of policies and proposals'. The concept of public involvement was introduced by the Skeffington Report (1969) and represented a reaction to the very vocal demands from articulate and organised groups for some say in the way in which their environment was being developed. Therefore most planning proposals are accompanied by exercises designed to gain opinions of the general public: exhibitions, public meetings and even public study groups, all of whom have an input at the preparation, survey and drafting stages and then at a subsequent enquiry stage if necessary. Alternative proposals are available, particularly in Structure Plans, but these can often be supported by conflicting groups of society. Participation is viewed with mixed feelings. There are those who see it as costly in planners' time and a delay on development brought about by a few people whose interests are affected while the majority of people remain apathetic. Others feel that participation can be used by the planners as the way of justifying their proposals because the public's proposals are all too varied. Participation is questionable in other circumstances particularly when the elected representatives and the planners remain at cross purposes with minority interests and over-ride them. A study in Croydon has shown how the local council comprises a large majority of business people with interests in the town centre. It was no wonder that an inner ring road and additional car parks around the centre were built despite opposition from residents in the affected area in the same year that monies for education were drastically cut back.

Study activity

Set up your own planning enquiry into, for example, a new shopping area or car park development, and each take a role of shopkeeper, councillor, planner, estate agent, local resident and ethnic group. Then debate the issues from those points of view. The same type of simulation is feasible for a housing scheme attached to a village.

Since 1979 there have been attempts to reduce the bureaucratic red tape in the Development Planning system of Britain in the interests of lowering public expenditure and speeding up the release of land for development, especially for housing. The grounds for holding up applications have been reduced. For instance development cannot be stopped until a Local Plan is completed and so developers can now pre-empt Local Plans if they obtain ministerial support, which in turn threatens the logic of the broader Structure Plan. Also the lack of adequate roads, sewage disposal and infrastructural facilities is no longer a ground for delaying planning applications. The **enterprise zones** established in 1980 where there is minimum planning control in order to encourage rapid industrial and housing development is another recent case of change in the basis of planning which we will examine in Chapter 7. Let us now look at examples of how governmental controls on growth have worked in practice.

Solutions to growth

Green belts, green wedges, green zones

Green belts as we saw in Chapter 2 have been one of the most enduring means of restricting urban growth. Since 1955 the green belt has been used as an instrument for restricting growth around most of our major urban areas, although they have not all been formally approved. There are three reasons for establishing a green belt: (i) to check the growth of a large built-up area; (ii) to prevent towns merging into one another; (iii) to preserve the special character of a town. Green belts are designed to restrict urban development although recreational uses such as golf courses and playing fields, mineral extraction and certain types of institutions, such as hospitals in extensive grounds, are permitted.

Study activity

Allocate each of the following green belts to one of the three categories above: a) London; b) Glasgow; c) Bristol and Bath; d) Oxford; e) York; f) Cambridge; g) Gloucester and Cheltenham.

The West Midland's green belt (Figure 6.3) performs several of these functions. It is a constraint on the spread of the conurbation, it separates Birmingham and Coventry, and it preserves the character of settlements such as Kidderminster. The plan also notes **green buffers** which are zones between two built-up areas.

Study answer

The green belts listed just now were a and b=(i), c=(ii) and (iii) for Bath, d–f=(iii) and g=(ii).

Several European cities use variations on the green belt theme and the variety can be seen in diagrammatic form on Figure 6.4. **Green wedges** penetrating the city, which can be continued across the city as **green corridors**, are used in Geneva. The **green buffer** has been favoured in the Ruhr area to separate Duisburg, Essen, Bochum and

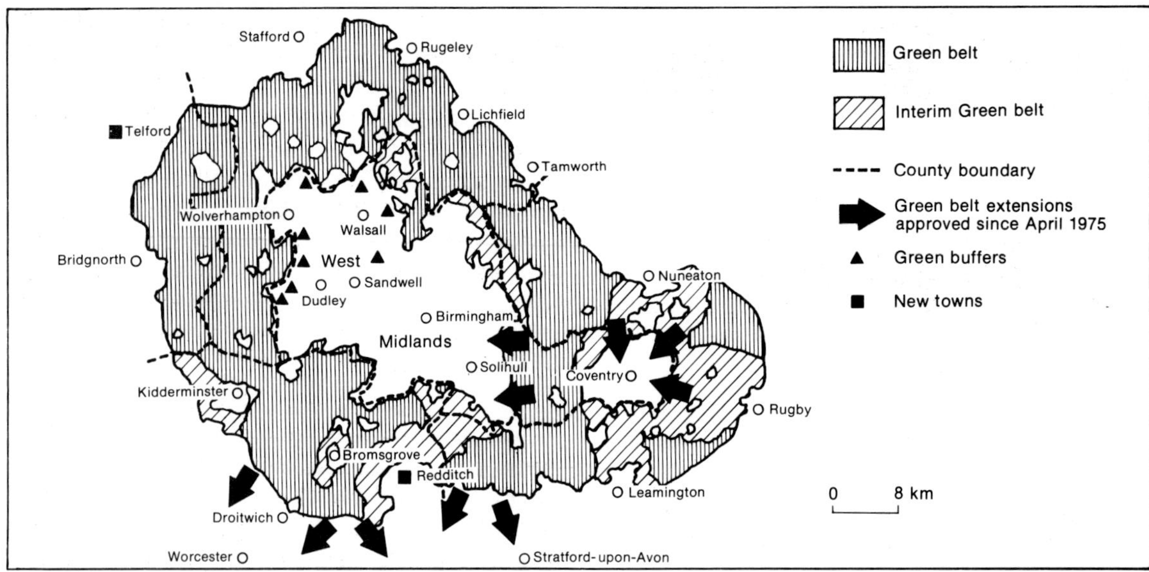

Figure **6.3** *The West Midland's green belt*

Dortmund from each other and from the northern towns. The **green heart** has been the famous solution of the Dutch for Randstad and the **green zone** is similar to the proposals for the Paris region.

Study activity

Choose an area of green belt. What types of land use are present in the belt? What types of development have taken place (i) in the belt and (ii) just beyond? (A copy of the local 1:25000 Land Use map would help in answering this.)

The big danger with green belts is that while they do restrict the outward spread of a city, they do encourage a process of leapfrogging development to beyond the belt. This is encouraged at an official level for instance by the designation of a new town such as Redditch or a desirable settlement just beyond the belt such as Leamington Spa (Figure 6.3). The very fact that villages in the green belt are unable to grow or have development in the gaps, ie. **infilling**, also means that their desirability often increases with the result that they can become middle class commuter settlements over a period of years and not villages in the old sense.

Study activity

1 How would you analyse a green belt village to see if it had changed its social composition to that of a commuter village? Undertake the exercise assuming that you would test it in the field. Perhaps having devised a method the exercise would make a worthwhile project if undertaken rigorously.

The new town

The **new town** is an essentially British solution to the problems of city growth which has been adapted in 67 countries and is an extension of Howard's garden city. They are free-standing, self-contained and socially-balanced urban centres planned to receive overspill population and employment in balanced proportions from congested conurbations. Many were designed around the principle of the **neighbourhood unit**, a small-scale residential unit or cell in which people feel at home. This is generally achieved by making the unit large enough to form the catchment of a first and middle school and to provide the everyday shopping and welfare needs of

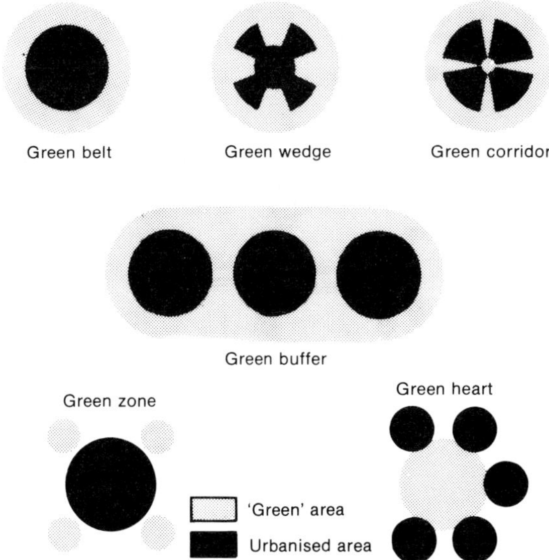

Figure 6.4 *A classification of 'green' planning*

the community. It tends to exclude through traffic and be laid out along Radburn principles.

Washington New Town (Figure 6.5) was designated in 1964 at the start of the second major phase of post-war new town development. It adopted the neighbourhood unit principle as an essential social planning component despite criticism of the principle in the earlier new towns, which noted that people's social activities are rarely totally within one neighbourhood. The neighbourhood units or **villages** reflect the structure of the local mining communities, some of which were included in the designated area. The villages are subdivided into **places** of 200–600 families where people have identity and these places are subdivided into groups of 24–50 dwellings, often around a common facility such as a shared garden or a playspace. There are several industrial areas, especially around the edge and along the motorway, often linked to a particular village. The road network threads its way through parkland which helps to delimit the villages. The centre, unlike the earlier new town centres, which were uncovered and not always pedestrianised, is a covered shopping complex with a bus station and associated car parks. An office district is adjacent to the centre, although there are problems in finding firms to occupy all the potential space.

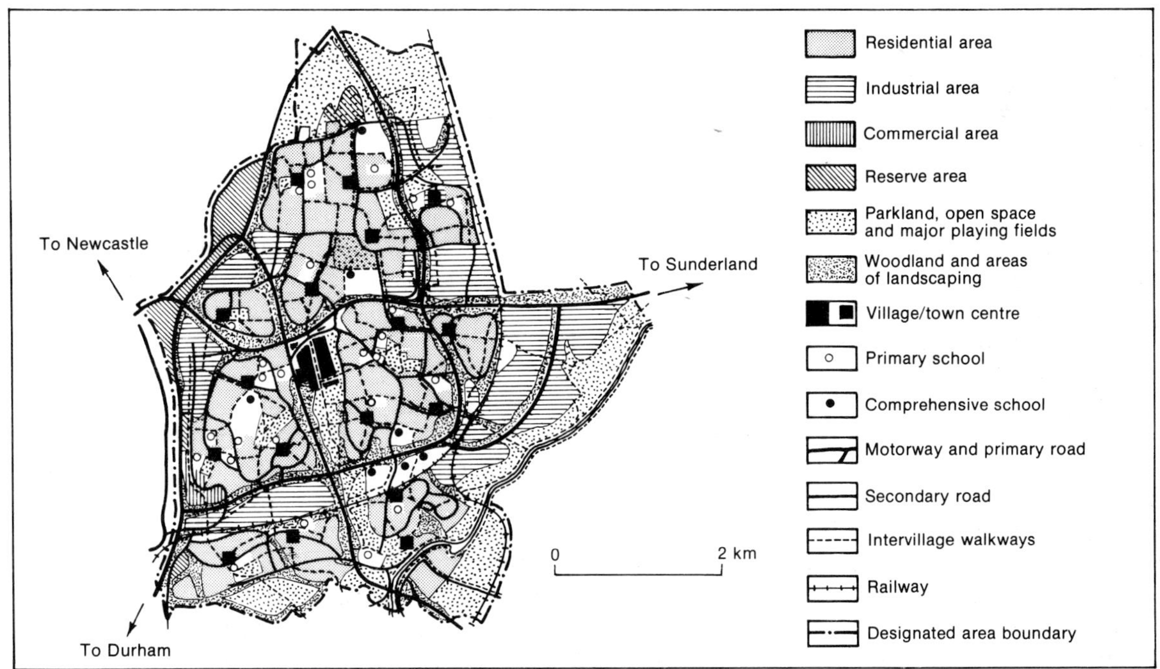

Figure 6.5 *Washington New Town*

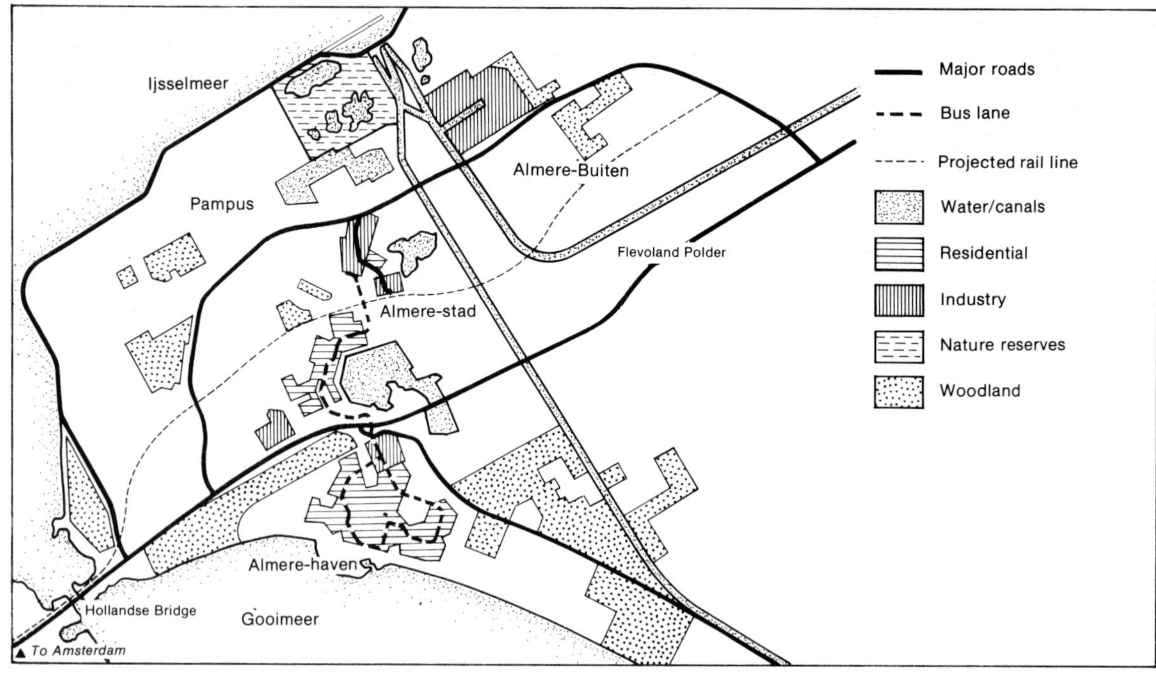

Figure 6.6 *Almere New Town*

The British new towns have been an outstandingly successful solution to the problems of city growth. Today they are home for two million people and 6600 firms. Only with the declining economic fortunes of the eighties and the changed policies towards new towns evident since 1976, has the overall pattern of successful development been slowed. Even so, it is the new towns in the less fortunate regions of the country with the less balanced employment structure, such as Skelmersdale, central Lancashire and Aycliffe/Peterlee, which have fared worst.

Almere (Figure 6.6) is a very recently developed Duch town in three major neighbourhoods at the south-western corner of reclaimed Flevoland, Almere Buiten, Almere Stad and Almere Haven. The neighbourhoods are larger. Almere Haven began accepting residents in 1978, three years after building commenced and by 1985 20000 will live there. Almere Stad, begun in 1979, will house 90000 of the planned target for the town of between 125000 and 250000 people in 2000. Two other neighbourhoods, Pampus and Gooi, are planned. It is accepted that many will live here and work in Amsterdam, a mere 20 km away, although 170 firms have been established and employ 4000. Public transport runs on segregated routes and cyclists and pedestrians also have their segregated routes through the town, with the result that the city has one of the most completely segregated, yet integrated, transport networks.

The new town has become a familiar part of urban growth policies in Eastern as well as Western Europe. Most studies have suggested that cities of approximately 110000 are easiest to organise and therefore the need to create new towns rather than to permit existing ones to grow was obvious. In addition, the socialist planners saw in new towns the chance to create urban forms that best embodied socialist principles of urban planning. The old towns developed under capitalism are not true socialist towns, even though the buildings have changed functions. New towns have been frequently developed in association with large industrial developments. Nowa Huta was developed outside of Cracow to house steelworkers. Similarly

Stalinstadt, later renamed Eisenhüttenstadt, was developed in the German Democratic Republic to house steelworkers. Halle Neustadt (Figure 6.7) was developed after 1964 to house the workers of the huge W. Ulbricht chemical plants at Leuna. It is a planned settlement to the south-west of Halle which accommodates 105 000 people. It is laid out in living complexes according to the principles which we discussed in Chapter 5.

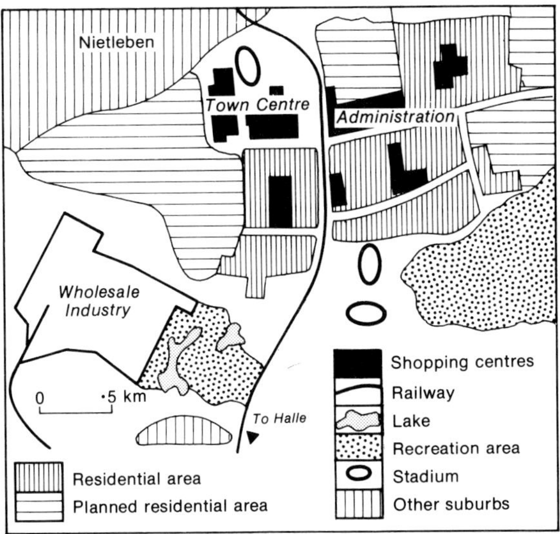

Figure 6.7 *Halle Neustadt*

The new town idea of balanced self-contained communities was also used in the plans for the Shanghai city region after its designation in 1958. The first of these was Minghang, 30 km south of the city and with the potential for port development on the Huangudiang river. The town's area of 1162 hectares was to have 650ha of separate residential neighbourhoods, 460ha for industry, transport and warehouses, which would be surrounded by parks (50.6ha). Schools, markets, clinics and shops were to be spread through the neighbourhoods, which was not dissimilar from British new towns. By 1970 it had a population of 70 000. At least 13 other satellite towns were designated in 1958 (Figure 6.8) and some reports speak of up to 70 satellite communities in the region today, of which the 13 on Figure 6.8 are the largest. As a result the population of central Shanghai in 1976 was 10.7 million or one million less than in 1953, but there were a further 5.47 million in the industrial satellites.

Study question

As we noted in Chapter 5, new towns have been built in Hongkong and Venezuela. Can you remember why they were built?

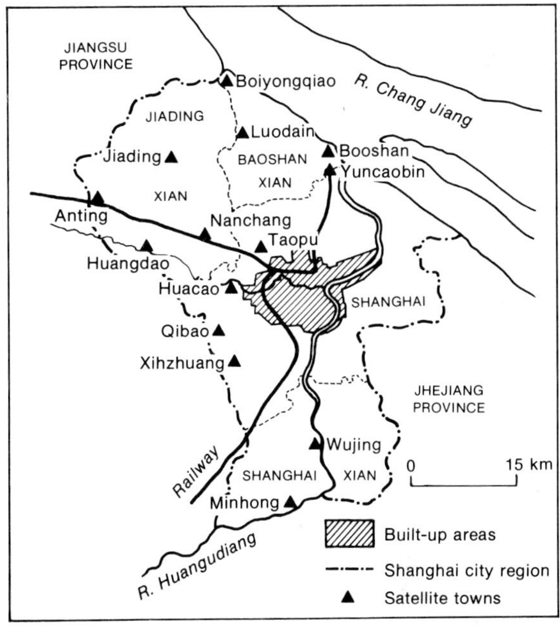

Figure 6.8 *Satellite towns of the Shanghai region*

Revision

1 Can you define: Radburn layout, ribbon development, indicative planning?
2 What are the differences between: garden cities, new towns and expanded towns?
3 What are the differences between: development plans, structure plans and local plans?
4 Draw a diagram to distinguish: green belts, green wedges, green corridors and green buffers.

7

The consequences of growth

The inner city

The spread of cities and the partially successful control of the outward growth of cities has produced in its wake a new and more serious problem which is generally termed the **inner city problem**. The inner city problem is a complex issue for which there are no simple explanations, no easily definable causes and more importantly, no cheap and easy solutions. It is therefore an ideal urban problem to illustrate how we cannot isolate problems totally from one another and how our own ideology and that of government will affect the outcomes which we prefer or propose to carry out.

Small Heath, Birmingham

In 1860 Small Heath was a tiny hamlet outside Birmingham, but by the end of the 1860s it had begun to develop following the establishment of factories along the railways and canals. Initially very poor quality housing was developed to house the workers. These **back to back** houses, which had poor sanitation and literally backed directly onto the adjoining terrace, were outlawed in 1871. The area developed from west to east through the latter years of the nineteenth century as a mixture of larger houses around the typical Victorian park and large tracts of terraced housing were built (Figure 7.1). The easternmost area was only developed in the 1920s when the Heybarnes council estate was built. Even in the 1920s the more skilled and affluent workers were leaving the area for the suburbs and some of the larger properties and terraced housing were filtering down to less prosperous families. Small Heath was thus the product of late nineteenth century urbanisation not dissimilar to the examples discussed in Chapter 1.

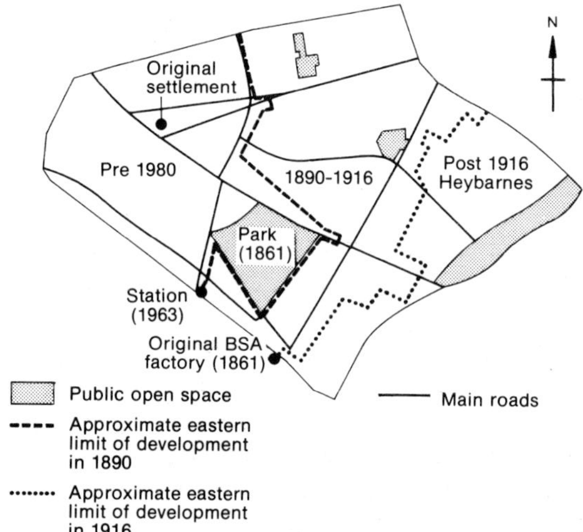

Figure 7.1 Small Heath: age of development

In 1946 Small Heath housed 50 000 people of whom half lived in the pre-1890 housing at densities one and a half times those of the eastern part of the area. Ten per cent of the population lived in the notorious back to back housing. It was the generally poor housing and environmental conditions of the area which caused Birmingham City Council to include half of the western part in its **comprehensive redevelopment** programme in 1957 (Figure 7.2). In this programme properties were to be demolished and the tenants of over 2000 rented houses were moved to properties on the periphery of the city. In their place a new high rise council estate was built and the council acquired other parts prior to renewal or redevelopment. Slum clearance, the removal of sub-

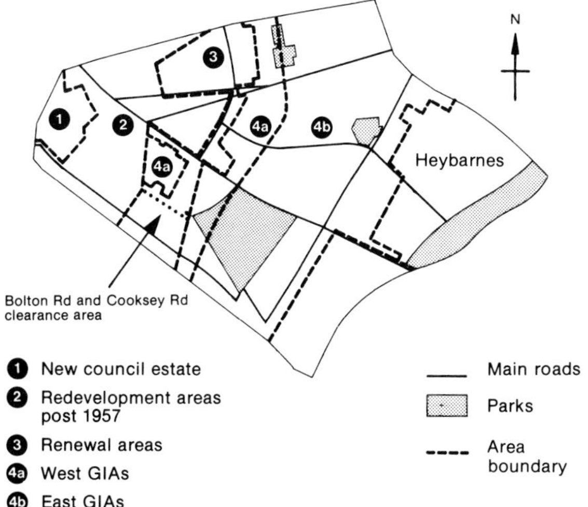

Figure 7.2 Small Heath: housing zones

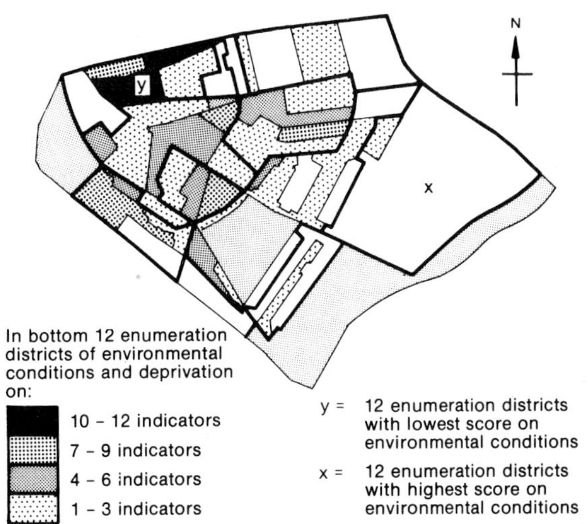

Figure 7.3 Small Heath: environmental conditions and deprivation

standard property, and the proposed Coventry expressway were the reasons behind the programme.

By 1975 the area had changed partly as a result of the early programmes and their effects on the built environment and partly as a result of developing social trends. The population had fallen to 32000 of whom 38% were immigrants from the New Commonwealth, particularly the West Indies and the Indian Subcontinent. Between 1960 and 1975 40% of the jobs in the area had been lost because the firms closed or moved out and those living in the area were increasingly employed in unskilled occupations. The average weekly income in households with one wage earner was £35 and only 14% of households had a weekly income of over £60. The average size of households was 3.42 persons compared to Birmingham's 2.97, and 25% of the households contained five or more persons. It was estimated that a quarter of the population lived in poverty and of these, four out of every ten were retired or dependent on a pension. Unemployment in 1971 was high (9%) and this had reached 20% in 1982. In 1971, 33 of the 75 census enumeration districts (EDs) were among the worst 15 percent of EDs in Britain on 8 out of 16 indicators of poor social and environmental conditions. 10% of EDs were in the worst 1% of British EDs on three indicators. Progress in improving properties through General Improvement Area (GIA) grants was slow (Figure 7.2) The council had acquired 10% of the houses which were among the worst because 40% lacked a bath and 60% were affected by damp. It was an area of declining socio-economic status where 'to be rich was to be able to pay the bills'.

The immigrants are relative newcomers to the area. The Asian community is Muslim and tends to stick together as part of the group's preservation and avoidance functions. (See Chapter 5.) They and the smaller West Indian community had moved in over the decade prior to 1975, replacing the higher income white population (higher here is relative!), who moved out. The children from wholly immigrant families made up one in three of all the pupils at school and a quarter of the pupils have language difficulties.

The picture of Small Heath at the time of the 1971 census was a bleak one (Figures 7.3 and 7.4). The areas are classified according to the number of times that they fall into the lowest sixth on the indicators listed in Table 7.1. The worst areas, 1 and 2, have high male and female unemployment; few cars; a large number of dependent children; most single parent families; most people per room; most overcrowding; most households

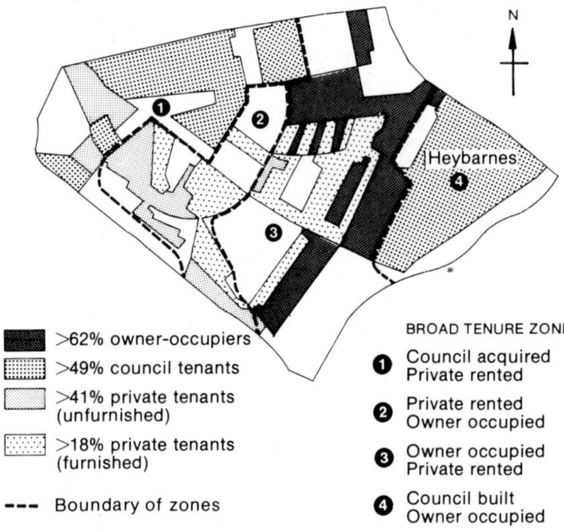

Figure 7.4 *Small Heath: household tenure*

Table 7.1 Indicators of personal deprivation in Small Heath

Census indicators of social and economic health 1971
1 Male unemployment
2 Female unemployment
3 Married women economically active
4 Male white collar workers (socio-economic groups 6–13)
5 Male unskilled manual workers (socio-economic group 11)
6 Households without a car
7 Population 0–14
8 Children 0–4 per 100 females 15–44
9 Single parent families
10 New Commonwealth population
11 Average persons per household
12 Average persons per room
13 Overcrowding (more than 1.5 persons per room)
14 Households sharing a dwelling
15 Dwellings with no fixed bath
16 Pensioner households
17 5-year movers
18 Employed in manufacturing

without a bath; and the smallest number of white collar workers. These areas represent **primary deprivation** or **multiple deprivation**, whereas the more varied conditions in areas 3–5 suggest that deprivation is noticeable on fewer indicators – **secondary deprivation.**

With an area like Small Heath as a cause for concern it is no wonder that the Prime Minister, Harold Wilson, announced the Urban Programme from the steps of Birmingham Town Hall in May 1968. He began a series of initiatives that have continued ever since. Small Heath is representative of the many inner city areas in Britain, although its ethnic composition is more akin to parts of London.

Explanations of the inner city problem

The **zone in transition** was a term coined by Burgess over sixty years ago for the area around the city centre and geographers ever since have been aware of this zone and the adjacent zone of working mens' homes. As we noted in Chapter 3 the concept of a **frame** around the city centre is a more recent concept which was based on further ideas developed in the United States in 1959. The model of the **core frame** is shown in Figure 7.5. It is notable that within the frame there are two activity groupings which we have seen in the Small Heath case study, although elements of others exist in Small Heath and elsewhere in inner Birmingham. Study Figure 7.5 and identify these two groupings. Further studies have described the subdivisions in greater detail but noting in particular the presence of **a sector of active assimilation** where the central area is growing with professional office conversions, trendy shops and improved desirable high quality housing; **a sector of passive assimilation** containing industry, wholesaling, low quality residences and flat blocks; and **a sector of general inactivity** close to the poorer housing, where factory closure and abandonment loom large (Figure 7.6). These studies do not say why

Study activity

Can the zones identified on Figures 7.5 and 7.6 be identified in a town or part of the inner city that you are familiar with? If there are variations or approximations to the model pattern can you explain them?

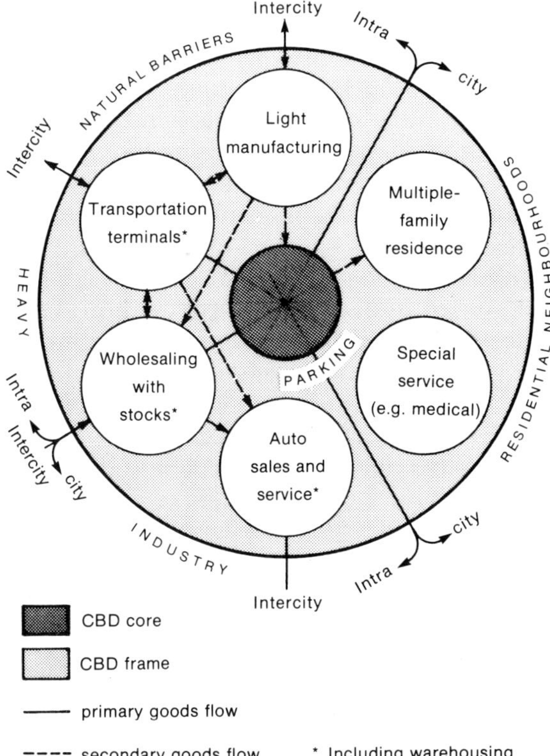

Figure 7.5 The core frame concept

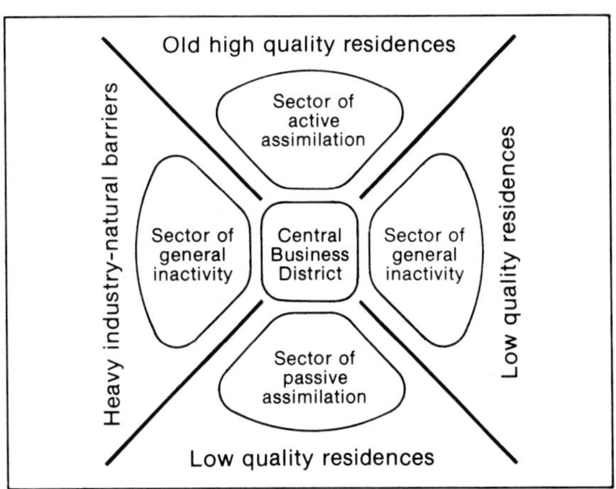

Figure 7.6 The zone in transition

there was a problem, although they illustrated the types of activity in the inner city.

There are a variety of explanations which exist for the demise of the inner city. Many of these do evolve around a basic debate as to whether the people are the problem or whether the places themselves are the problem. Both of these explanations naturally lead to certain solutions.

The study of Small Heath begins its analysis of causes by stating:
'At the root of them, however, is the unequal distribution of society's resources between different social groups, between individuals within those groups and between different geographical areas' (Unequal City, HMSO, 1977, p. 75).
People living in an area like Small Heath have poor access to opportunities from the beginning of life. The low socio-economic origins of the population tend to influence the length of time at school and a national survey showed that 15% of those of good intelligence from manual working backgrounds remain at school compared to 34% from the more middle class backgrounds. Then through their life and the family cycle they are unable to climb out of the conditions of low income and relative poverty of their birth. Deprivation is thus transmitted from generation to generation. These types of explanation have been called **the poverty cycle** and **the culture of poverty**. Obviously we have to ask why the steps taken over many years by governments through family allowances, supplementary benefits, and tax allowances have done little to alleviate the poverty problem in Small Heath. The agencies of government were deficient and so programmes such as the Community Development Projects which were begun in 1968 failed. The objective was to enable the multiple deprived population *'to pull itself up by its own bootstraps'*, but the twelve projects had all closed by 1978, partly because those charged with the task felt that they were tackling symptoms. For example, they helped in schemes for children rather than dealing with the root causes.

A second group of causes that we noted in Small Heath is the influence of inward and outward migration. Disadvantaged households have tended to concentrate in Small Heath as fewer skilled people arrive and more of the skilled population leave. In addition the concentration of New Commonwealth immigrants who moved into the area searching for cheap accommodation, aided the outward movement of the skilled white population. The immigrants settled in the privately rented accommodation and were more likely to purchase a home in Small Heath. The residential qualification (the need to live in an area for several years before qualifying) debarred most from council housing. It was the ethnic dimension to the inner city problem, together with the 1968 race riots in the United States, which prompted the initial government concern. This manifestation of unequal housing and migration opportunities was also used as an explanation of the British inner city riots in Brixton (London), St. Paul's (Bristol), Moss-side (Manchester) and Toxteth (Liverpool) in 1981. Decentralisation of the white population is therefore another explanation.

In an economic sense, it is not merely decentralisation but the deconcentration of industry from locations in the inner city which has been put forward as a cause for inner city industrial decline. Firms in the inner city have been subjected to pressures. First the locational advantages of railside and canalside locations have disappeared with road transport and the use of feeder lorries to rail depots. Therefore firms such as BSA no longer needed to be in Small Heath. Second, industrial processes have changed and the multi-storey factories of Small Heath are not ideal for modern assembly line production which is best accommodated in single storey factories. Third, many of the firms in the inner city have gone out of business because their product is obsolete. Not surprisingly, investors and developers are more interested in suburban locations as we saw in chapter 4. Sites remain derelict, or if reoccupied, they never employ as many workers. Others argue that industrial decline is a purely British phenomenon caused by the low investment in high technology over a period of years.

The inner city area is rarely attractive for office development and few property developers are willing to take the risk outside of the established nodes of office location in the central area and outer suburbs. There are exceptions, such as Stratford in East London, but, on the whole, new office sector jobs are rare in the most needy inner urban areas. Major retailing developments which can provide employment also avoid the inner urban areas in preference for the outer suburbs, although some schemes have taken place in our larger cities, for example, at the Elephant and Castle in London.

A further group of explanations have concentrated on the environmental causes of the problem. Empty and derelict factories and warehouses, undeveloped sites, abandoned wharves, all make ideal sites for filming the latest cops and robbers series for television, but they do not encourage investment. Similarly declining quality of housing particularly in its external upkeep and the general lack of upkeep of the streets also creates the wrong image. Research on housing choice has shown how the majority of people are quickly deterred by poor environmental conditions. As with the cultural poverty explanation for the problem, the **environmental determinism** argument has led to a series of area based solutions which we will discuss later.

The final set of explanations for the inner city problem do serve to broaden the whole issue. Those explanations are based on the works of Marx and Engels in the nineteenth century and have been developed more recently by Harvey and Castells and consequently are called **neo-marxist**. Cities become the focus of the capitalist mode of production where goods are made for the profit of the owners by workers and the city is the location for the struggle between classes. Small Heath, Lambeth, East Glasgow, and Lodge Lane, Liverpool, are all the product of the class struggle and can only be understood as the direct outcome of the action of a capitalist economy. In order to increase profits, firms have moved out. In addition, national and local government which have provided help for people in these areas, no longer have enough money from taxes and rates on companies and individuals to provide support and so decline and conflict are inevitable consequences. Therefore the inner city problem cannot be isolated; instead it must be seen as a national problem, the product of the nature of our economy and society. The explanation of the problems of Small Heath is therefore to be found in an analysis of the British economic and social system which is beyond the scope of this text.

Study activity

Can you recall the basic points of the *culture of poverty, migration, economic change, environmental* and *neo-marxist* explanations of the inner city problem? Do these explanations help you to understand the inner city area that you identified before you read this section?

Solving the inner city problem

Three reasons have been advanced for solving the problems of the inner city: (i) it is socially wasteful to abandon or destroy the investments in housing, transport and buildings made in the past; (ii) there are still a large number of people living in these areas and their welfare is a matter of national interest; and (iii) orderly change in these areas is surely better than allowing the stress to break out as it has done in 1968 in America and 1981 in Britain.

Area based policies have been favoured most in British policies. In 1969 local authorities were permitted to declare **general improvement areas** (GIAs) where funds could be made available for areas of up to 500 houses for play areas, landscaping and removing through traffic. It was tied with home improvement grants and therefore it was popular where there were owner occupiers, but not in areas owned by private landlords. These areas in Small Heath are shown on Figures 7.2 and 7.4. The policy tended to help the slightly better areas and between 1969 and 1973, 809 areas were declared and 242892 dwellings were improved as a result. GIAs were not only established in the conurbations (about a third), but also in other towns and cities (55%) and rural areas (10%).

In 1974 a further power was added, that of declaring **housing action areas** where better grants for house improvement were available, and where local authorities could force landlords to improve property. The policy was aimed at a gradual improvement in the housing stock in the areas of worst physical and social conditions, like parts of Small Heath.

A study of housing in inner Bristol in the 1970s has attempted to assess the area based GIA and HAA policies alongside grant aid for improvements. Grants for improvements to housing peaked between 1969 and 1973 and 60% of the grants were to inner city properties, but most were to the private-

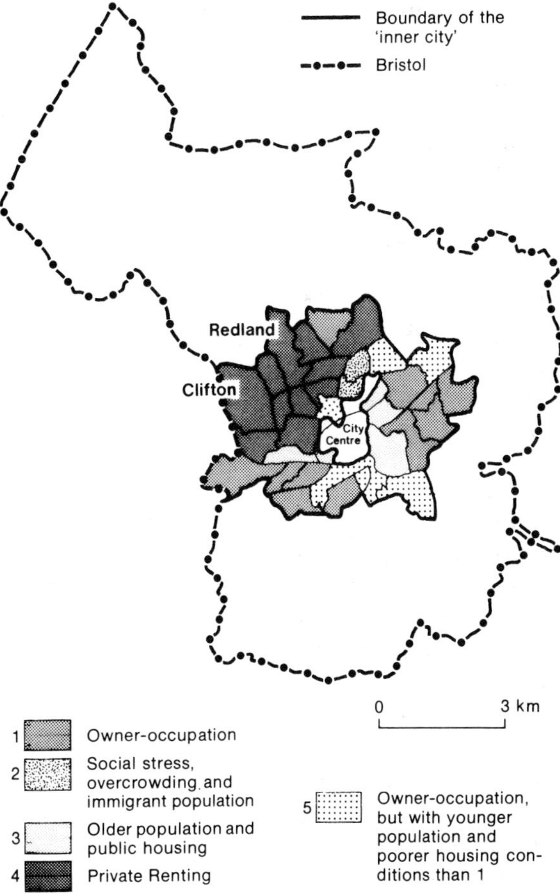

Figure 7.7 Housing areas of inner Bristol

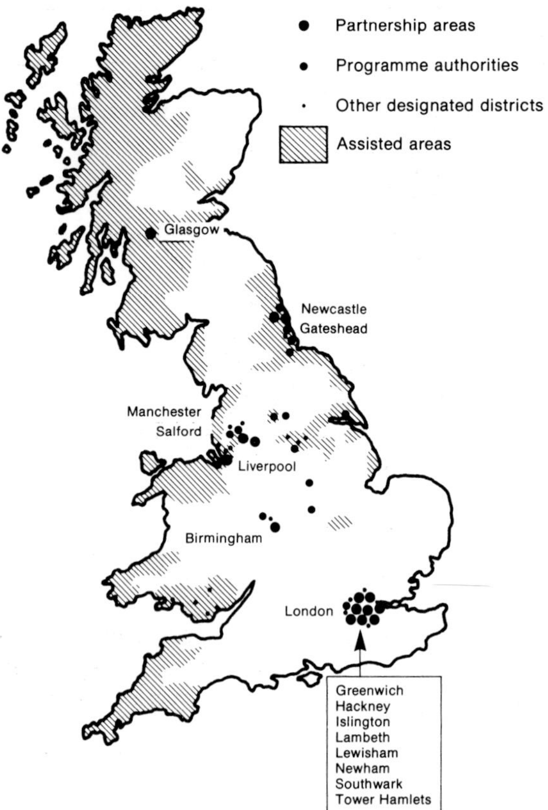

Figure 7.8a Partnership areas and programme areas in England and Wales

ly rented areas of Clifton and Redland (Figure 7.7), where landlords could push up rents to the young professionals living in that more desirable area of the inner city. The poorest areas only received 5% of the grant money. As costs have risen and controls designed to stop speculators have increased, so the number of grants has declined. Bristol had the potential to create 85 GIAs, but had only created 3 by 1974, containing 174 dwellings in the areas of social stress (Figure 7.7). By 1976 only 41 dwellings had received grants. The four HAAs were located mainly in areas of social stress (3), with one in the poorer owner occupied area. Again there was a potential to declare 25 areas with 5700 dwellings, but by 1979 only 602 dwellings had been dealt with. The cumulative result of the ten years was that it would take fifty years to improve all the dwellings in inner and outer Bristol in need of renovation.

The major reports commissioned by government, such as that on Small Heath, together with studies of Lambeth and inner Liverpool, were looking for area based solutions, although they concluded in 1977 that large cash resources needed to be ploughed in to regenerate industry. They therefore recognised economic rather than environmental causes for decline.

The government response to the inner city reports of 1977 was The Inner Urban Areas Act of 1978. This gave local authorities help in attracting industry and established a series of **partnership areas** and **programme areas** where various levels of assistance were available. Figure 7.8a shows the national distribution of these areas and Figure 7.8b the extent of the Birmingham area and the areas where the initial help will be concentrated. It is notable that although Small

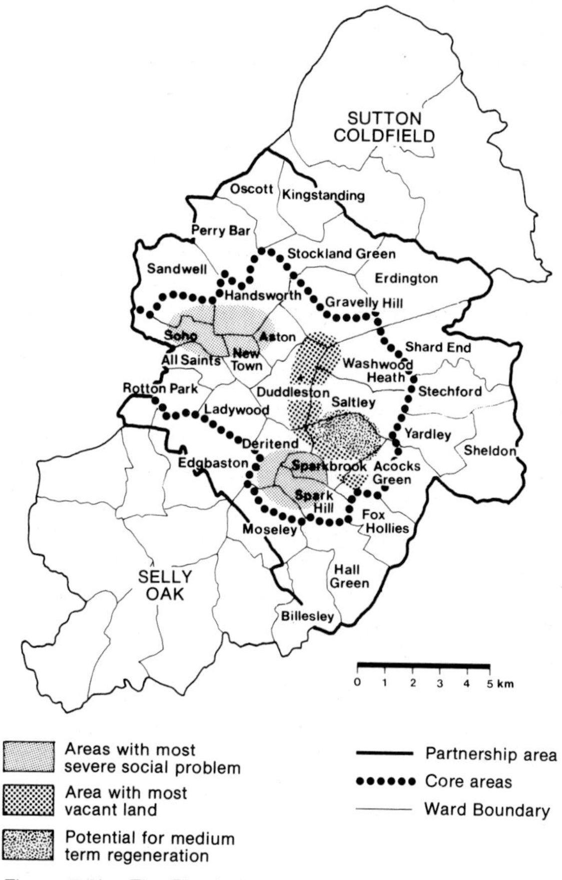

Figure 7.8b The Birmingham partnership area

Heath does not have the severe social problems of Handsworth and Sparkbrook, it does have large areas of vacant land and potential for regeneration.

Free Market Approach

Since 1979 there has been an increasingly obvious shift in policies for the inner city following the election of a Conservative government with a determined commitment to the free market philosophy. As a result urban aid tends to be granted where it will assist in the creation of wealth and where the private sector rather than local government is involved. It was suggested that the small effect of previous policies was partly caused by bureaucracy and the delays necessary to comply with planning law. Urban deprivation would be cured more rapidly if these brakes on progress were removed. The initial step in this direction was the creation of **urban development corporations** which could bypass the bureaucracy and produce rapid solutions without any public participation or real accountability to any particular authority other than central government. The first areas subject to the new approach were the London and Liverpool docks.

The second innovation to be introduced came in 1980 when the government adopted an idea of Professor Peter Hall to create **enterprise zones**. These are zones in urban industrial areas where small businesses can be introduced as an element in inner city revival. Eleven zones were designated and firms locating there would be exempt from rates and taxes; the rates will be paid by central government. Seven of the eleven zones (Figure 7.9) are near docks and most already have some form of assistance. They range in size from 320 ha at Salford Trafford Park on the Manchester Ship Canal to 57 ha in Wakefield. The zones in Corby and Hartlepool would not be characterised by most people as inner urban, although they are both in areas where the impact of major factory closures has brought about large rises in unemployment.

In 1982 a further nine zones were announced which were also not totally in inner urban areas. Nevertheless, they were in areas where major sources of employment had closed or been severely rationalised.

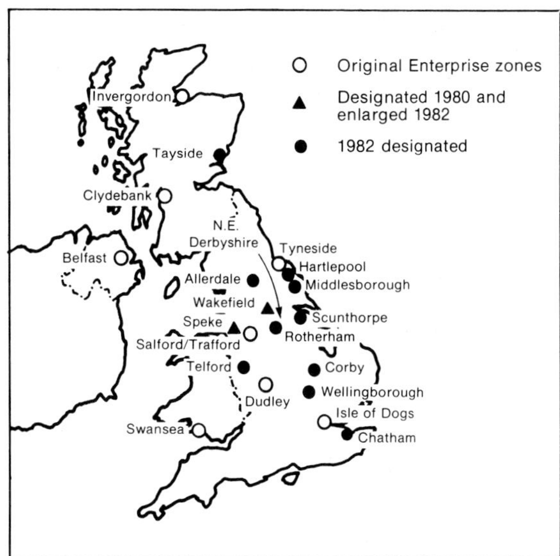

Figure 7.9 Enterprise zones in Britain

Study activity

Is there a GIA; HAA; UDC; or EZ near you? (Do you know what the abbreviations mean?). If there is, try using a 1:1000 or 1:1250 map to plot the obvious improvements to the townscape and the new activities. What help has the policy or policies been in redeveloping the area? What about the surrounding areas? Are they benefiting?

The urban transport problem

A second problem that results from urban sprawl is that of urban transport. The combination of the physical spread of the city in lower density suburbs; the dispersal of activity nodes such as shops and factories; the reduced attraction of the central city and increasing affluence has inevitably led to the growth of car ownership and the decline of public transport. The consequences are obvious for most urban dwellers to see during the morning rush hour: can you describe these?

The problem for modern city transport is basically how to provide for the variety of movement that modern life demands. Just examine the variety of destinations that your own family journeys to in a week and the timing of these journeys. The complexity of demand is very apparent. Cars are more flexible in their usage because they are door to door transport and enable the driver to vary the route and the timing of journeys. Yet most cars are four metres long, and, in rush hours, move into cities carrying a single commuter. A bus occupies the space of three cars yet carries far more people, but it is held up by the cars and has to follow a route which will gain the maximum income. Therefore routes can be tortuous and slow with many stops.

In general, as Table 7.2 shows, public transport journeys increase with city size whereas car usage increases in smaller settlements. In addition car ownership has spread through the social hierarchy. In 1979 36% of employers' households and only 2% of the non-skilled households had three or more cars. The figures for no cars were 4% and 14% respectively. Today it is the mobile who can choose where to live and who are not interested in public transport, so increasing the segregation between the more mobile households and the rest of society. The car is more valuable to people in the middle stages of the life cycle. Combine this factor with declining use of public transport and the reduction of public transport provision. It is the old, the young and the housebound, carless mother who are the probable losers.

Table 7.2 Method of travel and city size

Population	Percentage of journeys			
	Public Transport	Car	Walk	Other
250000 — 1000000	17	40	40	5
100000 — 249000	14	43	38	6
50000 — 99000	13	42	39	6
25000 — 49000	9	43	41	7
3000 — 25000	8	44	42	5
under 3000	7	55	30	8

Is it possible to make public transport more attractive? How can people in the low density suburbs be encouraged to be more socially responsible and use public transport? This is difficult when a large number of cars are provided by employers and therefore the full cost (ie. running, depreciation, tax and insurance) is not borne by the household. Public transport cannot compete in terms of comfort and door to door service and so it declines in the cumulative way suggested in Figure 3.15. Nevertheless, judicious planning has been undertaken to improve the attractiveness of public transport. Bus lanes and contra-flow bus lanes do help buses through congestion. Allowing buses on segregated routes, as seen in Runcorn, Evry (France), and Almere (Netherlands), is possible in planned new towns. Alternatively, buses that only travel on call, like taxis, such as 'Dial-a-Bus' which is used in Ottawa, are easy to introduce. Trams can run on separate lines and pass under or over crossroads, as in Bonn. City centre parking can be made so expensive that the alternatives are very attractive, as in Bremen. Alternatively, parking can be so limited that 'Park and Ride' schemes, such as that in Oxford, become viable. More expensive solutions are the building of underground routes such as the U-Bahn system of the German cities, which takes trams underground through the heart of Cologne or Hannover, or the Tyne and Wear metro system (Figure 3.16). Providing subsidies for public transport as in South Yorkshire or the ill-fated 1981 'Fares Fair' scheme in London are expensive to support but do appear to break motoring habits.

Study activity

Do you favour any particular form of urban transport? Debate the merits of the reforms and changes listed above with reference to a town or city. Who would favour each type of policy which you have suggested? Are there other solutions?

To be successful, transport needs to be planned and integrated into an overall system which functions. Several of the later new towns such as Runcorn (Figure 7.10) have been developed around the concept of a series of interdependent transport networks. Integrated transport is the feature of Newcastle where buses feed the metro stations, and in Munich and Hannover where car parks are close to tram and U-Bahn (underground) termini, and where suburban bus services fan out from key stations on the tram and underground networks. Much depends on who controls the transport in a city and how they see their duty to provide transport.

Study activity

To what extent are the various modes of public transport and private transport integrated in your home town? Can you explain why they are or are not integrated? Is it because of size of the town, the special needs of the town, or political control?

Who is getting what and where: the problems of provision

Under fives in England and Wales

There were approximately 3.4 million children under the age of five in England and Wales in 1979. Of these, only 162000 receive any help from local authorities towards their pre-school nursery education or playgroup activities. A further 495000 children are provided for by private and voluntary organisations, yet it has been suggested that up to 2.25 million need some form of pre-school provision. This has come about for several reasons to do with our changing attitudes to work and family life. The proportion of married women working has risen. In addition the proportion of working married women with children under five is increasing, especially in inner areas where the wife's wage is essential to supplement the husband's low wage or even lack of wage. Married women workers with small children are also more common among the professional groups and the more highly-educated households. The legal requirements for maternity leave have enabled women to retain a career through pregnancy. In addition, the number of single parent families have grown both as a result of separation and divorce, and as a result of voluntary single parenthood. The pattern of working mothers and single parents in London is shown on Figure 7.11 and the concentration of working mothers in the inner boroughs such as Lambeth, Newham, Hackney and Islington is very clear, together with large numbers in Hounslow and Ealing close to London Airport. The single parent families show a similar clustering in the inner city, but note the higher proportions in the

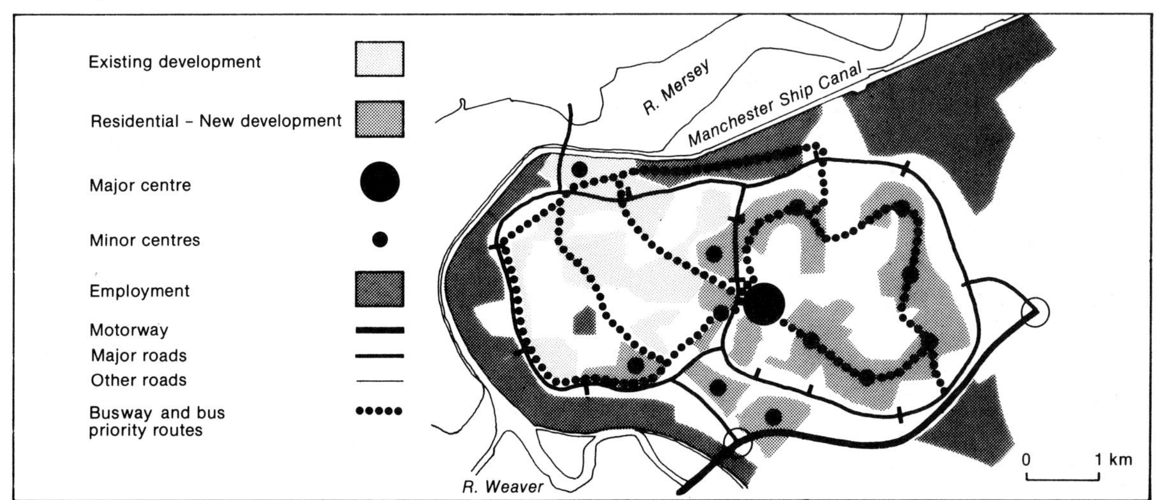

Figure 7.10 Runcorn's transport networks

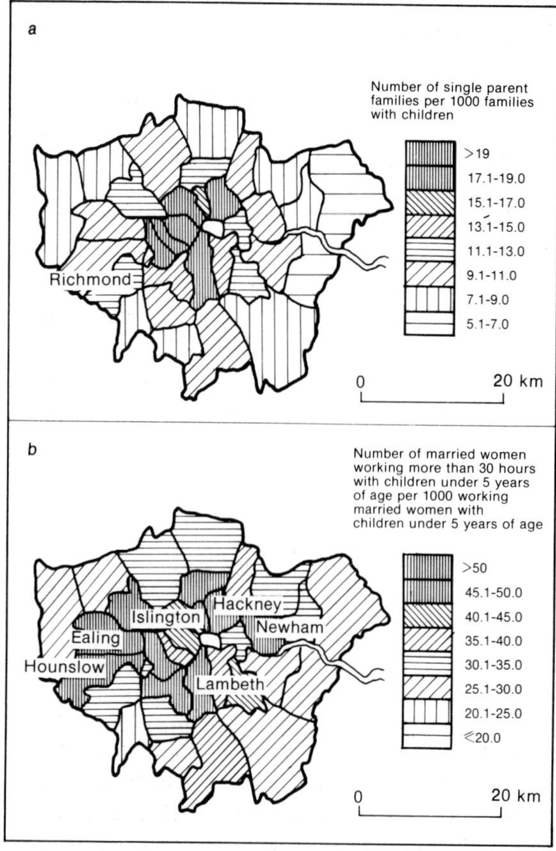

Figure 7.11 Single parents and working mothers in Greater London

borough of Richmond, in affluent south-west London. There is a further potential need for childcare facilities which exists among large families. These are also concentrated in certain districts (Figure 7.12). These variations in need would suggest that we ought to discover whether the supply of facilities coincided with demand. Geographers such as

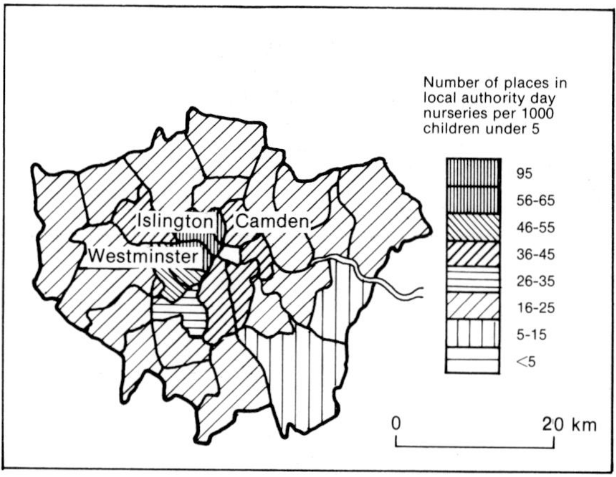

Figure 7.12 Childcare facilities in Greater London

Pinch have been looking at this type of issue, which is an attempt to see 'who gets what, where, and why'. It is looking at human welfare and has attracted the title of **welfare geography**.

Under fives in Southampton, Hampshire

In a study of pre-school provision Pinch has been able to show how provision varies both between cities (Table 7.3), and, more importantly, within a city. Southampton has a large number of nursery school places and playgroup places, but the level of provision per thousand population is not as high as Portsmouth. Childminders provision is poor compared with Andover and playgroup place provision is very poor compared with Basingstoke. The under representation of high income groups in the two big cities accounts for the day nursery provision with playgroups being more prevalent in high status areas like Winchester. In fact Hampshire has the fourth highest provision of voluntary playgroup pro-

Table 7.3 Pre-school provision in Hampshire

	Population	Day nursery places		Nursery school places		Playgroup places		Childminder places	
		total	rate/000 pop	total	rate/000 pop	total	rate/000 pop	total	rate/000 pop
Southampton	221700	90	0.40	367	1.73	1827	8.24	444	2.00
Portsmouth	191200	215	1.12	566	2.91	1524	7.97	644	3.37
Basingstoke	121000	30	0.24	58	0.38	2384	18.77	655	5.15
Andover	93600	—	—	52	0.28	1529	16.33	387	4.13
Winchester	91400	—	—	37	0.13	1512	16.54	175	1.91

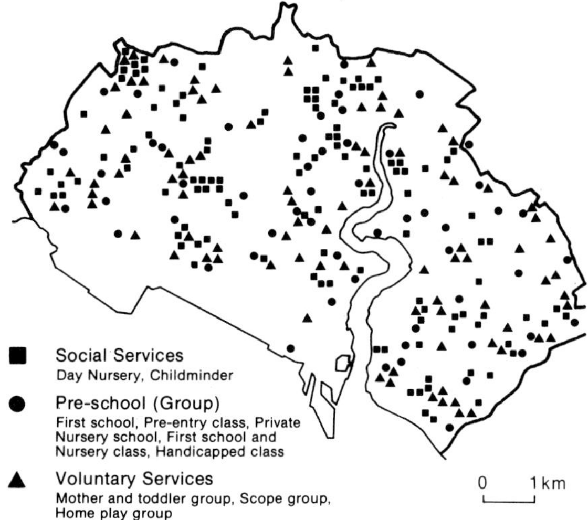

Figure 7.13 Pre-school facilities in Southampton

vision per thousand under fives in the country.

Within Southampton (Figure 7.13) there is a clustering of provision of pre-school facilities, yet first schooling facilities are evenly spread. Childminders are clustered in certain areas close to peripheral council estates, which suggests a **neighbourhood effect** where the presence of one minder in an area encourages others. Local authority day nurseries tend to cater for priority needs because of the lack of free provision and therefore their location is in the areas of greatest need in the city. Voluntary provision is partly orientated to areas where people can afford to pay, but also to the location of suitable halls. Pre-school services tend to be more associated with areas with a high proportion of professional and managerial workers and consequently a high proportion of owner-occupier households. Services for the pre-school age groups conversely are not found where there is a high proportion of unskilled workers or council housing.

Study activity

1 Hampshire is a Conservative controlled county. How might you expect this to affect the balance of local authority and voluntary provision for the under fives?
2 Table 7.4 shows the provision of voluntary playgroup provision for the under fives. To what extent are these extremes in provision related to the location of the local authority and political control?
3 In chapter 5 we suggested children were a muted group. How does our study of Southampton confirm that view?

Other possible fields of study that might identify variations in provision of facilities could be among the following. Health provision has long shown how the London health authorities receive more, and how a disproportionate share of London's resources were concentrated in the major teaching hospitals located where relatively few people lived. At the more local scale, you could look at the distribution of doctors, dentists and chemists, to see if they were easy for all to reach. Look at the rota of late opening for chemists and public transport provision. Can the non-car owning family get a prescription easily? Look at the council house sales which we studied in Chapter 5 and see if some areas are more saleable. Again ask yourself who is gaining in these areas. Are the local shops in different parts of town giving the same service? Contrast prices in a selection of small shops in different areas to see if there are variations. Who is most affected and where do they live? Conservation areas benefit some areas and some people more than others as we saw with gentrification (in Chapter 5). Unfortunately space precludes us from considering why areas are conserved and who decides what to conserve.

Table 7.4 Voluntary playgroup provision (number of places per thousand under fives)

High voluntary provision				Low provision			
Redbridge	(OL)	247	C	Rochdale	(GM)	66	L
Bromley	(OL)	239	C	Westminster	(IL)	64	C
Richmond	(OL)	214	C	Wigan		63	L
Hampshire		186	C	Doncaster		60	L
Bexley	(OL)	174	C	Tameside	(GM)		L
Dorset		170	C	Manchester		57	L
Cornwall		168		Hammersmith	(IL)	56	L
Gloucester		168	C	S Tyneside		53	L
Devon		159		Haringey	(IL)		L
				Walsall		50	L
				Knowsley		49	L

OL=Outer London IL=Inner London GM=Greater Manchester
C=Conservative control L=Labour control

Conclusions

We have taken three consequences of current trends in urban development in Britain to illustrate how geographers face up to the problems of modern society. No longer does the geographer just describe the problem and leave its solution to others. For many years geographers have been prescribing cures to problems by applying their knowledge in conjunction with planners. More recently, the geographer has become aware of the contributions of other subjects or disciplines to the solution of urban problems. The roles of economics (land values), political science (the nature of control), sociology (the nature of class, status), psychology (studies of behaviour), engineering (transport studies), statistics and computing (particularly for processing and utilising the mass of data available) are just as important as the spatial dimension of the geographer. Understanding, and, more importantly, explaining and improving the complexities of the modern city is **multi-disciplinary**; it is best performed by a group of experts. Even so, as we saw in Chapter 5, much will depend on the ideology and values held by those who study cities and those politicians who prescribe changes. Generally, local politicians are less than enthusiastic to be concerned with urban change because it takes longer than the four years duration of a local council for change to take place. Problems emerge over the years and solutions to health care provision, the lack of public transport, building car parks, or improving large areas takes even longer. City problems are not the place for the quick and easy solutions of the vote catching politicians; nevertheless, cities are the place where the complex issues of our society are to be found and have to be solved.

Revision

1 Can you distinguish primary, secondary and multiple deprivation?
2 How would you explain the problems that exist in the inner area of a city?
3 Debate the pros and cons of public transport subsidised by all through the rates and taxes.
4 Should urban facilities be provided equally across a city or should they be permitted to evolve?

All of these questions, except the first, are open ended and much will depend on your own values and beliefs. You may be moving towards your own personal views of the type of society that you would like to see in this country.